"Bruce Main writes out of a wealth of experience coming from years of ministry in one of the desperately needy cities in America. He is a master storyteller and biblical scholar, and in this book he is at the top of his game."

> Tony Campolo, professor emeritus of sociology,
> Eastern University

"Bruce Main has learned to look beyond the sacred page to discover what God is doing in the world around him. And what he has found in his looking is exciting stuff. This is a book for all of us who need help in 'spotting the sacred.'"

> Richard J. Mouw, president and professor of Christian
> philosophy, Fuller Theological Seminary

"Bruce Main has offered all of us a generous gift—the reminder to notice God at work through ordinary people living in extraordinary ways. The eyes of my heart have been opened and I am truly grateful."

> Dr. Stephen Macchia, president, Leadership Transformations, Inc.; author, *Becoming a Healthy Church*, *Becoming a Healthy Disciple*, and *Becoming a Healthy Team*

"Bruce Main is a storyteller. Always has been. That's why so many people, including me, have been drawn to his life-changing ministry in Camden, New Jersey. In *Spotting the Sacred*, Bruce turns his storytelling to the spiritual discipline of 'notice.' I didn't know it was a spiritual discipline either, but it is. Bruce tells us why and why we should embrace it as our own. I loved the book and encourage you to read it 'with your eyes wide open.'"

Jon R. Wallace, president, Azusa Pacific University

"The rich and wonderful gift of spiritual wisdom from Bruce found in *Spotting the Sacred*, written from the crucible of decades of serving Christ in an extremely complex urban setting, serves as a practical guide for all of us seeking to walk with God each day. Bruce has given the church a gift. Thank you!"

Peter Scazzero, senior pastor, New Life Fellowship Church; author, *Emotionally Healthy Church*

SPOTTING
the
SACRED

Noticing God in the Most Unlikely Places

BRUCE MAIN

BakerBooks
Grand Rapids, Michigan

© 2006 by Bruce Main

Published by Baker Books
a division of Baker Publishing Group
P.O. Box 6287, Grand Rapids, MI 49516-6287
www.bakerbooks.com

Second printing, August 2007

Printed in the United States of America

Library of Congress Cataloging-in-Publication Data
Main, Bruce.
    Spotting the sacred : noticing God in the most unlikely places / Bruce
Main.
        p.   cm.
    Includes bibliographical references.
    ISBN 10: 0-8010-6631-X (pbk.)
    ISBN 978-0-8010-6631-3 (pbk.)
    1. Christian life. I. Title.
BV4501.3.M247 2006
248.4—dc22   2006000296

Living stories worthy of notice, continually—
  Pamela Burgess Main—
    for letting me ride in your wake of spontaneity,
    thank you.

Contents

ACKNOWLEDGMENTS

For daily reminders of courage, hope, and perseverance, I thank the children, teens, and families of Camden, New Jersey.

For daily glimpses of commitment, sacrifice, and passion for justice, I thank the community of faith at UrbanPromise Ministries.

For the constant sounds of laughter and joy, I thank my children, Calvin, Erin, and Madeline.

For providing our family with a steady diet of divinely inspired moments and for her intuitive sense of God's prompting, I thank my wife, Pamela.

And to my friend, critic, and editor, Paul Keating: thanks for your willingness to review my stories.

My life is enriched by the witness of all your lives. May this book in some small way share this gift with others.

INTRODUCTION

> We must also keep our eyes open for the saints of our own culture. Their witness will be close enough to our concerns, or what should be our concerns, to leave us uncomfortable with our spiritual compromises.
>
> Charles Hoffacker

I wonder if you can relate to my dilemma: life has become somewhat of a blur.

Not that I am complaining. My life is full—family, friends, a job. But events and happenings seem to occur so rapidly that I have little time to ponder their significance and their meaning for my life. Information comes in torrents, not trickles. It is hard to know what to process, what to digest, and what—if anything—can add spiritual value to my life. I think I am becoming a little numb, especially when bombarded by all the bad news in the media.

Am I missing something?

If I take the time to scratch beneath the surface of the bad news or to reflect more deeply on the events of my life, will I have an opportunity to discover something more life-giving

11

and spiritually enriching? If I really take the time to *notice* what is going on around me, will I find opportunities to discover a glimpse of God's presence?

SISTER HELEN NOTICED

The front-page *New York Times* article was doubly depressing because it was about the city in which I work. Camden, New Jersey, was described in dismal and frightening detail as the most dangerous city in America: more murders, aggravated assaults, rapes, and violent crimes per capita than any other city. This small, postindustrial, East Coast city of eighty thousand had again beat out East St. Louis, Illinois; Detroit, Michigan; and Flint, Michigan, for the dubious honor. The reporter honed in on drug trafficking, gangs, and urban blight through paragraphs four, eight, and twelve.

But then, buried in the middle of the piece, the name Sister Helen Cole caught my eye. I blinked twice. Three times. Why was a Catholic sister being mentioned in an article about crime and violence? "A Nun's Blessing," announced the new paragraph, and then it continued to tell about a notorious neighborhood where there lives a nun attuned to another reality. The reporter talked of a woman who did not run from her neighborhood but instead walks with care and love. She had not shut herself away in a cloister; instead, to the surprise of the reporter, Sister Helen lives among the suffering and brokenness of her neighborhood, absorbing the pain of those who have lost themselves in the violence. She said, "I enjoy taking away pain. I hold out my hands and tell people, 'give me your pain, put it in my hands, let it go.'"[1] It is a process called *companioning*—an ancient practice of bearing the burdens of those who are overwhelmed with grief and sorrow.

12

Not only was the reporter amazed by Sister Helen's capacity to *companion*, but he continued by describing how this nun walks the streets of North Camden blessing the sidewalks where people's lives have been stolen through violence. Sister Helen sprinkles holy water, lights a candle, and prays that these defiled places become holy ground.

The idea of taking something ordinary (like a slab of concrete, a weed-strewn field, or a street corner) that had been tainted with evil and praying that it would again become holy seemed revolutionary to me. This kind of spirituality is a little outside my doctrinal box. The thought of a nun walking up and down the streets of my city, sprinkling water on bloodstained sidewalks, and praying for these places was an image of devotion radically new to my sense of faith. But there was Sister Helen expressing her faith in a unique and powerful way—an expression that not only caught my attention but also grabbed the heart and pen of a surprised *New York Times* reporter. After all, how many of us take the time to think about the spiritual dimensions of our neighborhoods? Most of us see little connection between the sacred and the cement. Sure, we'll quote a Bible verse that reminds us that "the earth is the LORD's and everything in it" (Ps. 24:1). But the notion that a strip of sidewalk can be a garden of life or death, a place for evil or good, is one that few of us would ever consider.

As I closed the newspaper, I had to wonder, was this usually unheralded woman a living parable of the good Samaritan? Was she a modern-day example of the woman Jesus noticed in the temple offering all she had to God? Was she a living, breathing, contemporary embodiment of Jesus's command to "be merciful" (Luke 6:36)? I wondered, had Sister Helen lived in Jesus's neighborhood, would he have elevated her as a person to notice, to watch, to emulate?

The article sparked something inside me. I felt a need to dwell on this unique life and to meet this Sister Helen Cole. I scheduled a visit.

Meeting Sister Helen

I have come to realize that often my deepest spiritual discoveries can be found in observing the lives of ordinary people who seek to practice their faith in ways that are authentic, truthful, and unheralded. The best sermons I hear are the ones lived rather than those spoken. Sure, reading books or hearing a great sermon may move me momentarily and provide more important information. But sadly, more information seldom guarantees that I will integrate those thoughts into action. When I read stories about courageous people, for example, I do not necessarily go out and act courageously. Courageous heroes of ancient times are safe for me. I can rationalize away my convictions because of their historical distance from my life. Neighbors and colleagues who act courageously, however, are not as easy to dismiss. Perhaps this is the deeper question with which many of us struggle: What really encourages spiritual growth in our lives? What really challenges us to internalize our convictions and thoughts and convert them into natural outpourings of love, compassion, and courage?

For me there is something profound about catching *a glimpse* of God's heart and nature expressed in the actual behavior of another in my presence, in my world. My problem is that I often miss those glimpses.

Benedictine writer Joan Chittister underscores this problem for me when she writes, "One can find it easy to go through life with eyes half shut and miss the angels and stars." How often do I miss those angels? I am afraid it is often.

That's why I almost missed meeting Sister Helen. Dread of the unrelenting tragedy and sadness of the daily news "half shut" my eyes to the possibility that buried beneath the city's accumulating detritus was something beautiful and life-giving—a life of someone listening to the heartbeat of God. And now that I had caught a glimpse of Sister Helen, I yearned to know more. I had gotten a glimpse of God's presence at work in the world, and I had an opportunity to see it up close. Within a mile of my office door walked a living source of spiritual encouragement, an opportunity to be shaken out of my complacency, and a chance to let a new image of devotion burrow itself a little deeper into my soul. I decided to act.

I knocked on the door of Guadalupe Family Services somewhat nervously anticipating my meeting with Sister Helen. The automatic lock buzzed and clicked. I entered and slowly walked up the threadbare carpeted steps to the second floor.

"Come on up," said a silver-haired, plainly dressed woman who was propped against the banister at the top of the stairs.

"I'm looking for Sister Helen," I said.

"I'm Sister Helen," she said while motioning me toward a cramped office that was cluttered with books on psychology, theology, and literature. Stacks of manila files suggested a heavy caseload and the absence of a secretary, yet a picture of Saint Francis smiled at me from over a desk. Pushed to one corner were baby toys, and games for children littered the carpet. It was an all-purpose room—part chapel, part study, part romper room, part counseling center. Never would the room be lauded in *Good Housekeeping*.

"Take this seat so you can look out the window," she said graciously. "I would like you to be able to see the sunlight on the tops of the buildings. It is really quite beautiful this time of day." I immediately felt at ease.

"We sisters of Saint Joseph are committed to *reconciliation* and *unity*," she informed me after we had moved past the introductory nice-to-meet-you. "We try to weave those ideas into all that we do."

"Yes, but how do those ideas work with families impacted by violence?" I inquired.

She smiled. "It is funny how things take their course. Fifteen years ago when I moved into this neighborhood, my work was terribly unfocused. I wasn't even sure why I was here. Then, senselessly, a young girl was murdered just behind the Pine Point School." She paused for a moment of reflection. "I went over to the family's home with my new business cards, and I invited them to call me if they needed any help. Sure enough, they called. Then others called. Soon I was listening and sharing in people's grief. This was the beginning of trying to bring healing to our community."

I learned that for the past fifteen years Sister Helen had served the children and families of North Camden with little fanfare. She worked under the radar of any media coverage and received only a stipend from her order to cover her most basic expenses. Helen found jobs for unwed teen moms, ran summer day camps for children on her block, confronted drug dealers, counseled broken families, and tried to absorb some of the pain of people who had lost loved ones to violence. She went on to tell me how embarrassed she was by the *New York Times* article. "The reporter wanted to meet some people who had lost family members to violence. So I naively introduced him to some of the people in crisis. The article was supposed to be about *them*. But I became the focus of his article. I think the reporter was just pretty cynical about faith and religious things and found me to be a curiosity."

"How do you stay encouraged?" I asked, trying to understand what nourished this woman's faith.

"Oh, it's our own little community here," she said with a delightful smile. "I live with three other sisters. We encourage each other. We are here for each other at the end of each exhausting day. We cry together, we laugh together, we pray. There's no way I could do this alone."

Then I realized why I had been compelled to visit her. Subconsciously I knew I did not need another sermon on sacrifice or commitment; I did not even need to spend more time reading Scriptures about being compassionate and loving. I just needed to dwell in the presence of someone who did not complain about how little money she made or her dire working conditions. I needed to be gently prodded toward the source of love by someone who was living in compassion and grace and loved God. More prayers about *my* needs for greater resources or better staff weren't it. What I needed was to be in the company of someone whose prayers were for the purpose of easing the pain of *others*. That was the message I needed. That was what I received.

I don't know how *you* find inspiration in the midst of your busy and chaotic life or what challenges you to move to a deeper place with God. Maybe it is a weekly church service or daily prayer and reflection. Maybe it is something else. I do know what is becoming increasingly real for me. When I try to live in a growing awareness of what is around me, I see glimpses of the God-life as expressed in the actions of friends, colleagues, strangers, and children. When I resist the temptation to live with my eyes half shut, I begin to see the possibilities of what it means to live out my faith authentically in the routine, the dismay, and even the chaos of daily life. Thus, I begin to find my heart being changed by the living testimonies of those in my midst.

But I need to look with intent.

I need to find the Sister Helens in my midst and thus be startled and amazed by the unfolding mystery of God's presence in the world as revealed through other human beings. And I believe that when this practice of *notice* is cultivated in my life and yours, we will find ourselves perpetually open to a God who never ceases to speak, to love, and to nudge us toward a deeper and more genuine faith. Instead of just grazing our way through life, we will learn to digest and taste the sacred richness of our experiences.

1

Beginning the Practice of Notice

The miracle of mindfulness in the savoring of ordinary life is the lens onto the sacred.

Dolores Leckey, *Seven Essentials of the Spiritual Journey*[1]

Have you ever driven in a foreign country—France, for instance? Well, there I was, rumbling down the A-86 toward Paris. My anxiety level was several notches off the charts. The Peugeots and Citroens were passing my Budget Rent-A-Car at 140 kilometers per hour. What really boosted my blood pressure was the thought of navigating the complex web of freeways at night to get to our destination on the other side of Paris. Of course, it didn't help that our three preteens, crammed shoulder to shoulder in the backseat with luggage on their laps, were tired and hungry after a full day of grudgingly being tourists. "How much longer?" moaned my ten-year-old every few minutes.

I clutched a Coke in my left hand and juggled my Michelin map on one knee, straining to see the tiny type. (Why do they make the print so small? Maps are read when traveling at sixty-five miles per hour under a low-voltage car light, in traffic jams, or on some desolate road.)

The man in the tourism office at the last stop had told me in halting English that I needed to go east on the *Periphique*. To my understanding, that was a bypass that circled the city. But trying to locate the *Periphique* on my map was like reading Tolstoy in Russian while jogging. Somewhere in the jumbled configurations of crossed red, green, yellow, and blue lines was the route I needed. I glanced up from the map just in time to see the *Periphique* exit sign. *Phew!* But I had one problem: there were not one but *three* exits.

"What's *east* in French?" I impatiently requested of my thirteen-year-old son, who was mesmerized by his Game Boy. He had taken two years of French.

"I dunno, Dad," he mumbled without glancing up from his game.

"I thought you got an A in French," I said as I slowed to a crawl. "Don't you know *east* and *west*?" The French motorists behind me were not happy. My wife was nervous. I'd have a word with Calvin's teacher, Madame Latrese, upon return to school in the fall, I thought to myself. "Please look it up in the dictionary," I called in desperation since I couldn't remember my high school French. To my horror I came to a barrage of new road signs. Exit name stacked upon exit name.

So what was the *Periphique*? I thought to myself. Was it the same as *Le Periphique*? Could it also be called the *Boulevard Circulaire*? Or was it the A-12? At least the French used the same alphabet as we did. I could not imagine the challenges of trying to decipher Arabic or Chinese script while speeding down a freeway. I turned down the radio and tried to rid my mind of distractions. Concentrate! Focus! I needed to slowly read every sign and try to differentiate the minute nuances between *Rue de* and *Route de la*, *Ave des* and *Quai's*, and the freeways labeled *A* and those labeled *D*. I was thrust into a situation where being totally alert to details was critical. Making a wrong turn would put me on some freeway that would take me away from my destination. With my minimal skills in French, the chances of engaging in a casual midnight conversation about directions with a congenial Parisian made that an unlikely option. I needed to find the right road. I needed to interpret the signs.

Finally, I saw the sign for *Boulevard Periphique* as my son was still fumbling for the translations of *east* and *west* in our English/French dictionary. He finally called out, with a heightened sense of excitement I had not seen since our last McDonald's stop, "East is *est*, Dad!" Under the exit name was the word *est* and confirmation that it led to the A-13—the next freeway I needed to find. I was heading in the right direction, and my son had learned a new word he could take back to Madame Latrese. Quickly I eased into the inside lane.

Noticing Life in the Fast Lane

How different are home, the familiar, the routine. I seldom need to notice the signs. I drive every morning from home to my office—left on Highland, right on 130, and another right at Federal Street. I turn on my radio, drink coffee, eat a donut, talk on my handheld phone with my old college buddy, and simultaneously think about my morning appointments. Paying attention to details is hardly important. The signs on the side of the road do not really matter, nor does the life that is taking place between the signs. When routine takes over, I don't really see what is going on around me. Just a momentary glance in my rearview mirror to make sure I am not cutting someone off.

So what is it about the unfamiliar that calls us to pay closer attention and has the potential of awakening us to the dangers of the routine? Sitting on the edge of one's car seat, eyes riveted for clues toward one's destination, is certainly a helpful metaphor for our life—especially if we want to live with a fuller awareness of what is happening around us. This rapt attention not only allows us to see the "road signs" more clearly but also helps us to see more of life taking place *between* the signs. More often than not in rushing blindly through the appointments, meetings, and encounters with other people, we miss opportunities to see and experience the presence of God in the ordinary aspects of our lives. We become content just skimming through life without ever pausing to consider that the events of our daily lives may have a deeper dimension—a truly spiritual quality.

Ray Bradbury's prophetic novel *Fahrenheit 451* picks up this idea as he describes a future world full of superficial people who live life at such a hurried pace that they can never slow down to appreciate anything. Since the release of *Fahrenheit 451* in the 1950s, many of Bradbury's images and ideas about the future have become chillingly real—wall-sized television sets that never turn off, our continual bombardment by advertisements, freeways with speed limits of seventy miles per hour, and people's infatuation with constant stimulation through entertainment, to name a few. The novel's main character, a man named Montag, earns his living as a fireman. The irony: in Bradbury's future firemen do not put out fires, they actually *create* fires. They burn books. Without books people lose their capacity to reflect on the deeper mysteries of life. By chance, Montag briefly encounters a young woman named Clarisse. Clarisse plays a critical role in helping Montag slow down and think about this life. During one of their encounters, Clarisse says, "I sometimes think drivers don't know what grass is, or flowers, because they never see them slowly." Montag is caught off guard. This kind of reflection is unfamiliar. "If you showed a driver a green blur, Oh yes! He'd say, that's grass!" Clarisse continues. "A pink blur! That's a rose garden! White blurs are houses. Brown blurs are cows. My uncle drove slowly on a highway once. He drove forty miles an hour and they jailed him for two days. Isn't that funny, and sad, too?"[2]

Most of us can identify with the notion of life as a blur. But is this how we are supposed to live? Are we to live life as distracted "skimmers" who never move slowly enough to really see anything? Fortunately, writers, poets, and artists remind us that in stopping to notice the ordinary, we often can experience a deeper reality beyond the superficial—something sacred. After all, is this not what all great artists do? Claude Monet calls us to look at— no, to *see*—in a different way water lilies and bridges adorned with light and life. With Van Gogh it's sunflowers. Georgia O'Keeffe painted her flowers huge so people would notice. Robert Burns calls us to contemplate the life of an insect in "Ode to a Louse." Leonardo da Vinci chooses weathered, praying hands and evokes a cathedral. Artists capture the beauty and meaning of life between the road signs. They call us to jump off the treadmill and *notice*.

But artists are not the only people given the opportunity to notice the deeper dimensions of life. Like artists and poets, people of faith are called to *notice* life, even if we are left-brain thinkers who find ourselves artistically challenged. As people created by God, we are called to become people who marvel in God's astonishing creation and celebrate its beauty. Our belief gives us opportunity to look at everyday items and encounters with imagination and creative insight—no matter how mundane they may seem. But whereas some artists may notice only the beauty of nature or the oddities of certain shapes and unusual lighting patterns, people who choose to view life through a lens of faith have the opportunity to discover a deeper sense of life's meaning. We can search for expressions of God's presence in *all* areas of our lives. By choosing to notice, we can discover that underneath our routines, our encounters with other people, our pain, and our disappointments, another drama is unfolding. It is a drama that beckons us to participate and seeks to inform our lives. It is a drama coinciding with the intentions and Spirit of God. It is a drama that is being acted out by ordinary people who are behaving in ways that capture the spirit of Jesus's teachings.

But routine, our daily habits, the speed of our lives have the seductive ability to lull us into complacency and diminish our ability to see that anything exists beyond the physical plane. And the more our days become depleted of spiritual meaning, the busier we make our lives. Busyness tends to provide momentary meaning and artificially abates our spiritual hunger. A hectic pace distracts us from our numbing routines and spiritual emptiness. We willingly stay on the treadmill because the thought of idleness frightens us. Consequently, we miss seeing the undercurrents of God's activity around us and fail to plug into this unique source of inspiration.

But routine and complacency are not all that prevent us from really noticing what God is doing in our midst and discovering the sacred plane intersecting with the physical plane. Distractions inundate us and blur our vision, prohibiting us from leading a life *noticed*. Many times I sit at my office in the center of a whirlwind of activity. Emails arrive incessantly. Phones ring and ring. Staff members interrupt with each impending crisis. At home, life hardly slows down: Children must be driven to soccer games—right now. Telemarketers know just when to invade the dinner hour. The Red Cross volunteer knocks on the door seeking a donation. Something, anything, insistently vies for our attention. Interruptions are continual. Most of us would like to experience a little contemplation and solitude. But we are caught in the cross fire of distractions and interruptions.

Few of us are exempt. Whether one is a stay-at-home parent who responds to the rapid-fire requests of children, or a teacher who juggles the personalities and needs of thirty energetic kids while grading papers and doing lesson plans, or a manager who supervises multiple staff, writes reports, and feels the pressure of making quotas, life has a fractiousness to it. We are saturated with information, distractions, and noise.

Is there no way out? Were we created to live at a pace so frantic and to endure so many distractions and so many interruptions? The mystics of antiquity would say no. I am sure the pious saints who fled the busyness of their worlds—to find solitude in the deserts and mountains—would contend that our modern life is way out of control. Those desert mystics Anthony, Macarius, Poemen, Theodora, Sarah, and Arsenius might advise us to struggle out of the raging river of the twenty-first century and seek a more contemplative life. Their wisdom has much truth to it. But many of us do not have that option. We have jobs. We have families. We drive on freeways, forced to keep pace. This *is* life in the twenty-first century, after all! Becoming a desert mystic hardly fits our future plans. Nor should it, necessarily. God needs people who live in the center of civic activity and who can craft a contemporary spirituality that provides and leads to emotional and spiritual health.

I must seek to answer these questions: How do I live in a fast-paced world yet develop a spiritual life that helps me see the continuous presence of God? How do I not become overwhelmed by the ordinariness and bad news of life and the multitude of daily distractions? Can a full, busy life become a source of spiritual encouragement to me?

I think it can. But this kind of life calls for a significant shift in our thinking about what is and what is not *spiritual*. To begin this quest we must learn to live as if God is at work in our midst *all the time* and, further, realize that the amount of time we "spend" in prayer has nothing to do with God's nearness and activity in the mix of daily life. The psalmist affirms this notion:

Where can I go from your spirit?
Or where can I flee from your presence?
If I ascend to heaven, you are there;
if I make my bed in Sheol, you are there.

Psalm 139:7–8 NRSV

The presence of God, claims the psalmist, is in our midst whether we like it or not, whether we are busy or idle. We can go nowhere without God's presence. As the German martyr Dietrich Bonhoeffer claimed, "God is the beyond in our midst." Or as the prolific German-American theologian Paul Tillich suggested, "God is the ground of all being." Whether in the most breathtaking vista, the dirtiest brothel, the most affluent corporate boardroom, the poorest mud hut in Central America, or the most "spiritually alive" church, God's presence can be found. Evidence of God's presence is not limited to certain pieces of "holy" real estate, such as churches, and certain appointed times, such as Wednesday night prayer meetings. (Perhaps this is why Jesus spent most of his time in places deemed unholy by his contemporaries— but we'll get to that later.) Evidence of God's presence and movement in the world can be found anywhere, at any time, if we choose to look.

Sadly, too many of us who earnestly seek to follow God spend a lifetime thinking that God's involvement in creation is connected to our doing. Consequently, we spend a lot of time feeling just plain guilt ridden about how little time we spend "with God." Yet this whole idea is misguided if we believe in the God of Psalm 139. God's presence and activity in the world are not conditional upon the success or failure of *our* solitude. Rather, our time in solitude helps to enrich our spiritual lives by creating a sanctuary-type environment where our eyes and our hearts can be opened to see what God is *already* doing in our midst, not where we can coerce God into acting in our midst. As our eyes begin to open and as we begin to cultivate the discipline of noticing, the opportunity arises for us to see that all of life can be "time with God."

But revising our models for spiritual growth can be difficult. I am reminded of this challenge each January at our first staff meeting after the Christmas break.[3] Often I will ask our workers to share some of their goals for the new year. Since our organization is Christian in mission, our committed missionaries often respond with sentiments such as, "I want to spend more time with God," "I want to carve out more time in my busy schedule for God," "I want to have more quiet times," or "I want to spend more time in prayer meetings." These are all admirable aspirations and important things. But implicit in their responses is the notion that a relationship with God is only strengthened outside of the *doing* of daily life.

Yet, ironically, often the same people seem to give me the same answers each year. Like promising ourselves to eat less and lose weight or to exercise more regularly, translating our intentions into sustained action is a very difficult process. Although these spiritual disciplines are helpful, they are not the only way to deepen our experience with God. They reflect a certain theological perspective—a certain tradition. It is a tradition difficult for those of us who have not chosen a monastic lifestyle. These goals reflect the idea that our most intimate times with God can only occur in isolation.

Once in a while a worker will say, "I want to see more of God's presence in my classroom," "I hope to experience more expressions of God's grace as I'm driving the bus," "I desire to capture glimpses of God's love at the laundromat and on the street corner," or "I want to become more acutely aware of expressions of God's heart in the lives of the children with whom I work." When we begin to embrace this vision for life, I believe we can begin to add a whole new depth to our faith journey. We can find new sources of inspiration, new challenges for holy living, and a deeper assurance that God is active in our lives.

Again, I am not discrediting the value of more traditional spiritual disciplines. Our devotional disciplines can be important, nourishing, and restorative. But we need to realize that simply living *in* the world means *we are already spending time in God's presence*! If we truly embrace this idea, then instead of looking for ways to significantly change our life patterns by building in uninterrupted times of solitude, we can begin to discern how to live more attentively in the *midst* of our active lives—each moment. In the words of the French monk Brother Lawrence of the Resurrection, we begin to "practice the presence of God" wherever we find ourselves. This is a difficult yet exciting step.

A New Way to Live

Our culture has influenced us to see, hear, and notice certain things and ignore others. We tend to notice temporal things like new cars, consumer products that will improve our lives, and bargains in the department store—isn't it amazing how we can notice a discount? We notice people's faults and sometimes enjoy poking fun at those faults. We notice people's shortcomings and failures and find enjoyment in watching them fall from their perches. We notice trends and fads instead of things that have an enduring quality. We notice successful people yet fail to notice that behind the veneer of confidence and certitude are often brokenness and dysfunction.

As people who desire to live more intently in tune with God, the challenge is to retrain our eyes, our hearts, and our ears to see life differently from what the world puts on our platter. When we begin to see life differently and more deeply, I believe we will find ourselves being challenged to live more faithfully, passionately, and intentionally as a witness for God in our world.

Fiction writer and theologian Frederick Buechner is on the right track when he claims that Jesus possessed this ability to notice God's presence in the ordinary stuff of life. Buechner writes, "All his life long, wherever Jesus looked, he saw the world not in terms simply of brokenness . . . but in terms of the ultimate mystery of God's presence buried in it like a treasure buried in a field." He continues, "And sometimes even in the midst of our confused and broken relationships with ourselves, with each other, with God, we catch glimpses of that holiness and wholeness which, no matter how buried and unrecognized, are still part of who we are."[4]

Jesus refused to view life simply on a physical plane. Jesus looked beyond the bad news of his day, caught glimpses of what God's reign looked like in the world, and then called others to notice. Those acts of notice became sources of revelation and instruction for those who followed Jesus. Those glimpses of God's mysterious presence in the broken and ordinary places of life became living parables and illustrations for how God desires people to live. And these living parables have continued to reach across the centuries and instruct people who look to the Christian Scriptures for guidance on how to live in ways that capture the heart of God

Just as God was active in Jesus's day, God continues to be active in our day. And like Jesus, we are called to begin the process of excavation by unearthing the buried and unrecognizable glimpses of holiness in our midst. We are called to live a noticed life.

2

JESUS AND THE PRACTICE OF NOTICE

I have long been fascinated with the domestic nature of Jesus' spirituality. Time and time again in the Gospels, Jesus embraces the most ordinary of circumstances and places, finding within them rich sources of spiritual meaning. . . . Jesus spends the largest part of his time in the most everyday settings—homes, neighborhoods, and marketplaces—identifying and responding to the presence of God.

Simon Carey Holt[1]

The lens through which Jesus viewed life was different from that of those who followed him. Throughout the Gospels we meet a Jesus who practiced the discipline of noticing people who acted in ways that gave expression to God's heart in the world. Whereas the religious types of Jesus's day were often blinded to these expressions of faith, gratitude, compassion, contrition, courage, childlikeness, and love, Jesus drew attention to these curious acts because they were snapshots of another reality—a God-infused reality that he desperately wanted his disciples to see and practice in their daily lives. These ordinary people in ordinary places were where Jesus found living examples for his followers to emulate. By noticing, Jesus showed us that all of life can be saturated with spiritual meaning.

Like so many people, I have subconsciously (and consciously, for that matter) compartmentalized my life. I have my "spiritual appointments" (namely, church, personal devotions, retreats, and worship) when I am consciously looking for some kind of revelation from God—guidance, wisdom, and insight. And then I have my other appointments, such as board meetings, meals, teeth brushing, bill paying, doctors' appointments, and all the "distractions" along the way—moments when I am not exactly looking for God.

But Jesus models a different way of living life. The pattern of Jesus's life seems to indicate that God's presence is not limited only to the *spiritual* stuff. It was in the ordinary aspects of his daily existence that Jesus noticed these sacred snapshots—living pictures possessing a message capable of nudging people closer to a life bearing witness to God's intimate involvement in the world.

When I read the Gospels, I meet someone who does not compartmentalize his life between that which is sacred and that which we might deem as "secular" activity. Sure, Jesus had times of isolated prayer, times in the temple, and moments of teaching lessons about God—things we would deem "spiritual." But the totality of Jesus's life was infused with a spiritual quality. Jesus somehow experienced a sacred, mysterious dimension of life in the most ordinary aspects of daily life. Why was that? Was it simply because God's Spirit resided with Jesus in an extraordinary way—a sort of Spirit-filled buffer zone that infected everything within a mile of his presence? Did Jesus's divine nature uniquely give him the upper hand over the rest of us, giving him a kind of X-ray vision into the realm of the spiritual? Or was it because Jesus, in his humanness, *chose* to *notice* and acknowledge this presence in every moment of his life?

I believe it is the latter. To argue that Jesus had an unfair advantage over his fellow humans is to succumb to the heresy that Jesus was not "really" fully human and not subject to the same human limitations, pressures, and restrictions that you and I face each day. Many Christians believe that Jesus was a Six Million Dollar Man who turned his divinity on and off—using it whenever it worked to his advantage. Other Christians just idealize first-century Palestinian life and believe it was somehow saturated with a special spiritual quality.

Those kinds of theology is dangerous and are simply projections of our imaginations. And when we make these assumptions, we compromise one of the most critical of Christian doctrines: Jesus was fully human. Jesus walked dusty roads, took naps, ate food, got blisters, grew in wisdom, went to parties, and probably suffered an occasional headache. His world was fraught with political tension, violence, religious unrest, and poverty. Besides the obvious differences in technology and communication, the pressures of Jesus's world were as great as our own. Therefore, we must resist the tendency to romanticize Jesus and his world and must embrace the following reality: the man Jesus chose to live his life differently. He viewed life as a drama infused with expressions of God's presence in daily life—expressions that were waiting to be discovered and called into being through the act of *noticing*.

WHAT DID JESUS NOTICE?

Most Christians agree that in both the teachings and the life of Jesus we find truth lived—a truthful life displaying examples of how to live with an intentional bent toward a more God-centered existence. By trying to comprehend this truth and implement it in our own lives, we begin the process of becoming people who bear the new life of Christ in our lives. In order for us to move toward spiritual maturity, it is important that we understand how Jesus lived his faith differently from his religious counterparts. This insight will give us a deeper sense of how Jesus exercised the practice of notice in his own life and ministry.

Jesus's divergent approach to a God-centered life redefined the notion of holy living for his listeners and placed him at odds with the religious establishment. First-century religious leaders, as portrayed by the Gospel writers, were unrelentingly in conflict with Jesus. Those conflicts arose over doctrinal differences, views of tradition, and his supposedly "inappropriate" association with people who were ostracized from the religious community. The religious leaders in Jesus's day associated a God-centered life with the things deemed *spiritual*—the temple (the place where people met God), doctrine (holding to correct beliefs about God), and religious practices (living out a specific moral code). Jesus, on the other hand, did not center the entirety of his spirituality on things considered sacred. Although Jesus spent time in the temple, honored some aspects of religious tradition (he told one man he healed to be checked by a priest, for example), and told his followers that he came to fulfill the law and not abolish it (Matt. 5:17), we discover a Jesus who exercised his relationship with God in ways and in places that were *not* deemed spiritual by those who maintained the religious system.

It was on the dusty roads, in the graveyards, and in the outer regions of Galilee that Jesus spent time discovering people who embody a life reflecting some aspect of God's nature—in places that were generally looked down upon by the religious establishment. It was in the Gentile regions and territories like despicable Samaria—places where orthodox Jews would never enter—that Jesus found living illustrations of faith-filled people. Oddly enough, these people whom

34

Jesus upholds as examples of faith are often the very people the religious leaders refused to endorse as full participants in the religious life of the community. It was the sick, the ostracized, the child, the woman—those on the lower rungs of society—whom Jesus held up as a witness to God's movement. Other than the synagogue ruler who groveled at Jesus's feet, asking Jesus to heal his daughter, can we think of one situation in the Gospels in which Jesus actually celebrated and affirmed the "God-like" behavior of a religious leader? Outside of affirming the military leader who begged for the healing of his son, did Jesus use any prominent political figure as an example of love, compassion, faith, or sacrifice? No. It was the people on the margins of society whom Jesus *noticed* and pointed our attention toward. And like a detective looking for traces of divine activity in the most ordinary of everyday situations, Jesus called his followers to see those traces and then challenged his disciples to take notice—*to do likewise*!

These everyday examples of people living faithfully attracted the attention of Jesus. And in our pursuit to embody the characteristics of Jesus in our own lives, it is the ordinary people living in extraordinary ways who should attract our attention. Just as Jesus used these living examples to challenge his disciples to live differently, we should be challenged to live differently by the snapshots of people who reflect the heart of God.

Unfortunately, many of those who desire to live in greater communion with God would say that these snapshots of faith, courage, compassion, and gratitude that Jesus saw do not exist in our world today. "You don't know my circumstances!" says the salesperson. "The people I work with are just ordinary, boring types!" Or "My life is in such a rut that nothing extraordinary ever happens." That might be true. But I think we are more often blind to what is taking place in our midst. We have been taught to look in all the wrong places or not to look at all. We spend our free time watching "reality" TV and the dramas of other people and fail to see the wonder of what is taking place within the sphere of our own lives. Our eyes must be retrained *to notice*.

Jesus lived differently from the religious types of his day. He redefined what it meant to be spiritual by living a life that challenged what his contemporary culture meant by *spiritual*. By breaking away from *spiritual places* and *spiritual people*, we meet a holy man who provided a new paradigm of spirituality by noticing expressions of God in places most of his contemporaries believed were void of God's presence. Consequently, Jesus offered hope to those who spent most of their time in spaces and situations that his world (and the church, for that matter) would deem void of God's activity. He affirmed that a life rich in God's presence was not limited by geography or demographics. He affirmed that the relentless, creative involvement of God's presence was everywhere and never ending.

ARE WE SLEEPING?

Perhaps the one advantage Jesus had over most of us is best articulated by the great French mathematician Blaise Pascal. Pascal believed that the greatest enemy not only of prayer but also of the whole spiritual life of a person was *inattention*, *drowsiness*, and *complacency*. Using Jesus's encounter with his disciples in the Garden of Gethsemane as an example, Pascal called this inattention "the Gethsemane Sleep." When Jesus needed his disciples to be in tune with the overarching drama of what God was doing through him, sadly, tragically, his disciples slept.

Pascal claimed that prayer is really being awake, attentive, and intensely open. Prayer is not simply closing one's eyes and reciting a list of nonnegotiables to God. Prayer, rather, is an awareness of what is going on in one's midst. For Pascal, sin was described as anything that destroyed this attentiveness:

pride, self-will, self-absorption, double-mindedness, dishonesty, sexual excess, overeating, overdrinking, overactivity of any sort. They all destroy, he would maintain, our capacity to be attentive. Thus Pascal believed that the whole purpose of prayer was to move us out of our "Gethsemane Sleep" and into a life of openness and attention to the things God is doing in our midst.[2]

We are therefore admonished to become people who *notice*. But with our appointment-paced, overstimulated lives, we too often live in a type of Gethsemane Sleep; we are reluctant to wake up. Thus, we need the Spirit's guidance to reveal those areas of our lives that rob us of becoming attentive and open people. Pride, self-absorption, and overactivity all deaden our ability to evaluate the sacredness of our lives. And so we keep stumbling along in a mediocre life that is spiritually empty. I am reminded of the Senegalese proverb that so aptly summarizes our dilemma: "The opportunity which God sends does not wake up those who are sleeping." The Gospels provide an account of a man who was truly awake. We must learn from his example.

Beginning to Notice, Beginning to Digest

The model for spiritual growth familiar to many of us often centers on what some would call the *banking method* of learning. We believe that if we just read more, listen to more sermons, or memorize more Scripture, we will deepen our spiritual walk. Although there is truth and importance in this idea, we must realize that spiritual growth is not just about pouring more content into our heads.

As we read the Gospels, we see that Jesus did not subscribe to this model of teaching either. When the disciples did not understand something, Jesus did not just give them another lecture, ask them to memorize more of the Torah, or cram more theory into their minds. Rather, Jesus realized that their old paradigms and presuppositions needed to be challenged. Often the disciples were blinded to seeing the world as Jesus needed them to see the world. Consequently, the disciples needed a new way of seeing. The disciples needed new images to illustrate what it meant to live as people who express the presence of God in their daily lives.

This is why Jesus continually pointed out to his disciples the holy actions of ordinary people and said in essence, "Did you see that person? Did you see that act? That is faith in action! That is love in action! That is gratitude in action! These are signs of God's work in the world." Jesus needed his disciples to notice because they were supposed to embody these aspects of God's witness in the world. Like a good teacher, Jesus prepared his students for life after his departure.

But the disciples stumble along in spiritual blindness throughout the Gospels. Actually, of all the Gospel writers, Mark is the most ruthless at pointing out the disciples' inability to see what Jesus needs them to see. In Mark 8, after witnessing a series of miracles, the disciples still fail to see beyond the physical dimensions of life. In a sharp rebuke, Jesus says to his beloved disciples, "Are your hearts hardened? Do you have eyes but fail to see, and ears but fail to hear?" (vv. 17–18). It is no accident that Mark follows up on this rebuke by sharing the story of the blind man at Bethsaida—a man who was blind but then is given vision by Jesus. In essence Mark underscores the disciples' need to be healed of sight. The disciples need to become people who can see the intersection of the spiritual and physical planes.

This is where we must begin.

We must begin with the confession that we do not notice all that we need to notice. We must commit ourselves to living with the kind of attentiveness needed to see God's presence in the actions of those in our midst. It is when we begin to notice as Jesus noticed, that we will find our daily routines becoming richer, deeper, and more life-enriching.

It is when we begin to notice, as Jesus noticed, that we will find ourselves challenged by the "living sermons" we hear and see from unlikely preachers.

This book is about learning to notice. In the following chapters I provide a framework for living a life of notice. In each chapter I highlight one moment *noticed* by Jesus in the acts of ordinary people he encountered during his public ministry. These encounters obviously impacted the life of our Lord and will hopefully call you and me to notice some of these same themes in our own interactions today.

Fortunately, Jesus did not simply use these acts of notice to expand his own sense of self-awareness. After identifying these unique expressions of God's movement in his travels, Jesus called his followers to *digest* these experiences and to draw spiritual nourishment from them. By drawing attention to these acts, Jesus called his followers to reflect, ponder, and make spiritual sense of what was taking place in their midst. Yes, Jesus taught through the spoken word. Yes, Jesus told stories. But Jesus also affirmed that the God-life was present in the actions of ordinary people, used these God-present actions as illustrations for spiritual growth, and then challenged his listeners to digest these observations and use them as motivation for acting more God-like in the world.

This is the challenge Jesus leaves to his followers today. We must *notice*. We must *digest* what we notice. And then we must allow these holy experiences to shape our hearts and minds and influence the way we live.

3

LOVE NOTICED

"Leave her alone," said Jesus. "Why are you bothering her? She has done a beautiful thing to me."

Mark 14:6

An Episcopalian bishop being interviewed on television caught my attention. The talk show reporter had asked the traditional questions about church, faith, and the national spiritual climate. Finally, the host asked, "If you were to summarize faithful Christian behavior in one or two sentences, what words would you use?"

At this the old bishop paused, thoughtfully tugged at his beard, and said with a slight twinkle in his eyes, "Christians are people who love *wastefully*."

What?

Love and *waste* in the same sentence? Oil and water had more in common. Bishop or no, his words at first blush didn't seem compatible. After all, shouldn't love be dispensed wisely, sparingly? Perhaps frugally or cautiously—but wastefully? Never.

I wondered later why I had such a strong, visceral reaction to the bishop's words. Was it perhaps because I had been raised in a home where *waste* was a bad word—on par with four-letter words? Sure, that must be it, for my folks were thrifty people: always recycling bottles, tin cans, newspaper, wrapping paper, and scrap metal—long before recycling tubs arrived at the end of our driveway. Dad stacked a month of the *Times* want ads, opinion pages, sports sections, and Sunday cartoons, bundled them with saved pieces of twine, then drove them across town to some church basement so the Boy Scouts could earn a few pennies by turning them in for recycling. Mom too. She saved even the pickle bottles so she could use them for canning blackberries from the summer crop. Socks with holes were never thrown out, just darned and then worn for another year.

But my favorite recycling memory involves my school lunches. I didn't have a fancy action figure lunch box like other kids had; instead, I would take my lunch to school in a *used* Oreo cookie cellophane bag. I was then expected to return the bag home so that it could be used the next day. My proud all-time personal record was four months with the same bag!

Growing up in a home where "waste not, want not" was like a silent benediction to our family prayers left an indelible impression on the inner crevasses of my psyche. Would it take ten years of psychotherapy to erase the tapes? The thought of waste was enough to stop the act from ever happening. Throwing away any reusable object was a treasonable act. Wasting was not part of our family culture.

So hearing the bishop talk about loving *wastefully* conjured up all my childhood memories. How come the venerable bishop didn't know that love, like everything else, should be given out sparingly, not squandered? Love should be spent like a hard-earned paycheck. And shouldn't love be given to those who have earned it, to those who have groveled for forgiveness, or to those who know generosity when they see it? *Love should not be wasted!* Do you think that just maybe the bishop had touched something primal within me?

But my bishop friend was saying something completely different. He was reminding me of what Jesus taught when he asked, "If you love only those who love you, how are you different from the sinners?" (see Luke 6:32). He was reminding me of the Jesus who healed even those who did not thank him, who advocated forgiveness for those who had wronged him. And Jesus loved with waste.

A Dinner Guest to Notice

Dinner that particular evening was different from others—at least for Jesus (Mark 14:3–9). At Bethany, Jesus noticed something. A woman came into the room and anointed his head with a very expensive perfume. The reaction of those in the room—presumably the disciples—was anger.

They were *indignant* over such waste! What about the poor?

And they were pleased that their indignation was justified. That woman's actions were way over the top. Behavior like that was embarrassing. And from a cost analysis basis, there were much cheaper substances to use and much better ways to spend the money. It was just plain wasteful, and that woman certainly needed to be reprimanded. Was there no decorum left?

But Jesus? Rather than jumping on board with the group's disgust, Jesus noticed the woman's behavior for what it really represented: *a beautiful thing*. He challenged his listeners to focus on what was important. In essence, Jesus stopped his disciples in their tracks and said, "Oh, men, men, you've missed it again! You've traveled with me for three years, and you still don't get it, do you? You've failed to see the heart behind the act!" Then Jesus said that the act of this unnamed woman (someone they all knew) would be immortalized—an act of wasteful love would be eternally linked to the preaching and teaching of the gospel. Who would have suspected then that this dinner party would still be talked and written about around the world thousands of years later?

Mark's placement of this event in his Gospel was also impressive. In the first two verses of chapter 14, Mark described how the chief priests and the teachers of the law were looking for a surreptitious way to arrest Jesus. Mark wrote that Jesus was surrounded by religious leaders with malevolent intentions. In the tenth verse Judas went to the chief priest to betray Jesus. What Mark presented are two frightening examples of self-serving, hypocritical, and deceitful behavior. Mark contrasted these negative examples of religious leadership with the woman's example of true discipleship.

One preacher captured the essence of hypocritical religious leadership when he said, "Those who know ten times more about the Bible than the rest of us do not necessarily love ten times more." The religious leaders knew God's words. Judas lived with *God's Word*. But neither lived the message with hearts of love.

Mark provided a vivid example of faithful discipleship in the midst of two very negative examples. Against the backdrop of self-centered and corrupt hearts, Jesus pointed to this very ordinary, unpretentious woman and said, "Look! Notice! Pay attention! This is how a God-saturated heart is to act." By placing that woman's act of exuberance between the two "bookends" of deceit, Mark made sure that her act was not easy to overlook. Jesus noticed her and lauded her, and Mark made it a point to heighten the importance of her act by placing it where he did.

CONTEMPLATING LOVE

Jesus's affirmation of this woman's act of *wasteful love* connected deeply with his own life and mission. After all, why was Jesus crucified? Was it because he traversed the Galilean countryside promising eternal life to those who could recite the four spiritual laws? Of course not. I would argue that the reason Jesus was crucified and killed was that he *loved wastefully*—his love could not be contained by the social and religious structures of his day. Because Jesus did not love within the parameters of what was religiously and culturally acceptable, he was a threat to those in power.

When Jesus expanded his mission to Gentile territory in Mark 8, he did something a good Jewish prophet would never do: he demonstrated that God's love was not limited to people of Jewish origin—his love could not be contained by geography or nationality or heritage. When Jesus traveled through Samaritan territory, he demonstrated that his love could not be contained by ethnic barriers—good Jewish prophets were not to associate with Samaritans. When Jesus engaged in conversation with the Samaritan woman at the well (John 4), he demonstrated that his love was not restricted by the gender barriers of his day. When Jesus invited children to come to him, he showed his listeners that his love could not be contained by social barriers. When Jesus healed on the Sabbath, it was an act of love that could not be accepted by tradition. Jesus's love, compassion, and concern were not contained by social boundaries and arbitrary borders. Jesus loved lavishly. Jesus loved expansively. Jesus loved wastefully.

The liberating power of the resurrected Jesus was not simply for the purpose of providing a way for humans to spend eternity with God. The liberating, redeeming power of the resurrected life is so that our often small, careful, cautious, boundary-abiding, barrier-honoring, crusty, fear-filled hearts can be freed to love with excess, lavishness, and vulnerability. This is good news!

And that woman who anointed Jesus at Bethany embodied this kind of love—a kind of love that will change our neighborhoods, our schools, our churches, and our world.

Unfortunately, I find myself too easily identifying with the disciples in this story. I would have been angry right along with them at their evening meal. My list of world-relief organizations and important social causes would have justified my anger. Or, if anger did not consume me, I would pass off her actions as being silly, embarrassing, and inappropriate for a dinner party. My pride would blind me from noticing what I needed to notice—the heart behind the act would have been missed.

But the investment of the "wasted" perfume continues to increase its value as it speaks to each new generation of believers. This event gives us an opportunity to do better than the disciples. The woman at Bethany reminds us that people who love without limitations capture the essence of a Jesus-following life. "Dear friends, let us love one another," proclaimed John, "for love comes from God. Everyone who loves has been born of God and knows God. Whoever does not love does not know God, because God is love" (1 John 4:7–8). Those who truly love, *know* God.

We must look in our midst and discover those who *love with waste*. And when we do find those who love in extraordinary ways, we must laud their acts and do likewise. The late Mother Teresa of Calcutta said, "We cannot do great things. We can only do small things with great love."

STORIES OF LOVE NOTICED

You might be more apt to identify with the disciples in the story than with the woman who loves with waste. Practicality may govern your actions more easily than loving people who do not "deserve" your love. Sure, we may embody the virtues of kindness, goodness, and politeness (at least most of the time). This is important, but Jesus calls us to a higher form of love—a dangerously vulnerable, lavish, extravagant type of love. I confess, this kind of love is difficult for me to exercise. It helps to see this wasteful love *lived* in front of me. Seeing real people love this way seems to push me toward exercising this counterintuitive behavior. Here are a few stories of wasteful love. May they enrich your spirit and challenge your heart.

Every Monday Morning

Love is patient.

the apostle Paul
1 Corinthians 13:4

The panel discussion entitled "What My Family Taught Me about Life" had wound down to a yawn when the moderator wandered onto the hazardous road of asking for questions and comments from the audience. A stately gentleman rose.

"I'd like to share a story," said the white-haired gentleman as he struggled to his feet.

The restless audience members shifted in their seats, trying to get comfortable. Some coughed. Others looked at the decorations on the ceiling, hoping that the older man wouldn't drone on too long. It was lunchtime, but the facilitator affirmed the man's request.

"A number of years ago," the man began haltingly, "my eldest son, Tom, left for college. I remember the time as if it were yesterday."

Oh, this was going to take a *long* time.

"His mother and I helped pack our station wagon with Tom's few belongings and headed for the University of California. It was the early seventies, and Berkeley was a turbulent campus. But I had confidence in our son."

Relaxing into his story, the man told about how his son finished his freshman year with stellar grades. "He was a premed major," he said, "just like his father. I couldn't have been prouder." Everyone responded with a dry smile.

47

"Well into Tom's sophomore year, I received a call from the dean of students. 'Were you aware that your son has dropped out of school?'" The father paused for a long moment. Was he going to cry?

"With some anger," he finally continued, "I assured the dean that my son had not dropped out of school! And, no, we hadn't talked to him in three weeks, but that wasn't unusual. He was busy. We wanted to give Tom space to grow.

"He said, 'Your son has not attended class in over a month. His roommates have not seen him.'

"My nurse cancelled my appointments. I got on a plane to Berkeley that night," continued the father. "I talked to Tom's roommates and friends. I discovered that Tom had been spending a lot of time with some strange cult group on campus. He had gone away on a weekend retreat. His roommate told me, 'We haven't seen him since.' I began to panic.

"For the next few weeks I searched for my son, talked to the police, filled out a missing person's report, frantically pressured the cult members who were recruiting around campus. Nothing. *I was numb*. My son had vanished. His mother was falling apart. *Was he dead?* I wouldn't even think about that.

"For two endless years there were no phone calls. No letters. No contacts. The inklings of hope I shared with my wife in the months following the disappearance had died. Only old photographs remained, and dimming memories . . . and questions."

The lecture hall was silent. We were all enthralled by this point.

"But every Friday I would get up at four in the morning and write my son a letter. Pretty much I just told him that I loved him. I shared little stories about what our family had been doing the past week. I wrote about how his absence left a void in our family. Then I would address the envelopes General Delivery, Berkeley, California, and postmark them."

48

Everyone in the room had a vision of that faithful father alone in his study, scribbling out handwritten letters to one he loved deeply—week after week, month after month. What must it have been like to post those letters? Would they find their way into the hands of the son? The trash? Had they already? What persistence!

"One Monday morning," he continued, "I was in my office. My secretary buzzed me: 'Doctor, there's a call on line one.'

"'Yes?'

"'Dad, it's . . . it's Tom.'

"'Tom?' Was this a cruel joke? But it was his voice! It *was* Tom!"

Tears were rolling down the cheeks of almost everyone in the room. What had started as an impersonal monologue in a roomful of strangers had become intimately personal. No one there was exempt from the pain of a broken relationship. All had experienced the heartbreak of a wayward child, a deep friendship gone awry, or a lost family member.

"'Dad, I'll explain everything later,' Tom rushed on, 'but first I want you to know something important: every Monday morning for the past two years I took a bus to the Berkeley post office and asked if there was any mail for me. I was so confused and so depressed. I had made up my mind that if there was no letter from you, I would end my life. But Dad, thank God, every Monday morning there was a letter waiting for me . . . from you."

"Every Monday morning there was a letter waiting for me . . . from you." That was the line that stuck to all who listened. We all conjured an image of this father, like a desperate member of a search crew, casting a lifeline into the dark abyss each week with no guarantee that it would get in the hands of his son. But he did it anyway. With just a prayer and a flicker of hope, this humble example of persistence sent letters of love with nothing more than a trace of faith that they might fall into the familiar hands of his lost son. *And they did!*

Few of us remembered what the panelists—those social scientists, psychotherapists, family counselors—at the conference shared in their presentations. But the father's story vividly remains. I left the room thinking about the people I may have given up on—those who struggle and need from me the persistent, unrelenting love expressed in constant acts of caring. Patient love . . . a love that proves itself over time . . . love that is not conditioned upon one's response. Had I been like Tom's father?

The apostle Paul knew what he was writing about when he penned to the church at Corinth the words "Love is patient." He followed that with the promise that love never fails. Can you believe it? Love that is patient *cannot fail.*

Oh, and yes, Tom broke from the cult and finished Berkeley and medical school. According to his father, they ended up in practice together.

Sometimes continuing to love a person might seem like a waste. We may measure the "worth" of our time and "practicality" of our investment by the kind of response we receive. Fortunately, the love Tom's father demonstrated was not dependent upon the recipient's response. Perhaps the essence of wasteful love is that we just love for the sake of love. Is there someone you need to love wastefully?

Carpenter Counseling

A true act of love, unlike imaginary love, is hard and forbidding. Imaginary love yearns for an immediate heroic act that is achieved quickly and seen by everyone. People may actually reach a point where they are willing to sacrifice their lives, as long as the ordeal doesn't last too long, is quickly over—just like on the stage with the public watching and admiring. A true act of love, on the other hand, requires hard work and patience, and, for some, it is a whole way of life.

Dostoyevsky, *The Brothers Karamazov*

I usually don't make it a habit to get marriage counseling from carpenters who come to fix things around my house. Pete was the exception—not just because he had a leather tool belt strapped around his waist, a hammer in his hand, and two days' worth of stubble that made him somewhat menacing. It was because he had a blunt, forthright manner and offered his advice without solicitation. To make matters worse, that morning he had caught the tail end of an argument between my wife and me.

"I want to tell you something," he said gruffly. "You just blew it with your wife!" The hair stood up on the back of my neck. I wanted to slip out the back door, but he had me trapped, and there was an edge of exasperation in his voice. "Oh, sure, I also blew it—too many times—with *my* wife. And that's why I'm now on my second marriage. But I learned." He didn't take a breath. "For instance, the other day my wife wanted to go to the beach," he began seemingly in the middle of an idea. And I was, incongruously, glad I wasn't paying him by the hour.

"I *hate* the beach," he said, making it sound like a curse. I wondered where this monologue was headed. "There is nothing I hate more. I hate the sand in my toes. I hate just sitting there doing nothing. I *like* being busy. But I went to that beach only because my wife asked me to. *She* wanted to go. And y'know what?" Pete smiled. "Later that day she told me how very much our going to the beach meant to her—especially since she knew how much I hated the beach."

Well, I was beginning to feel the early pangs of conviction, because the current spat I was having with my wife was all about my resistance to doing something that was important to her. It was simply that I didn't want to change *my sacred schedule* to accommodate hers. Also, plainly and simply, I just didn't want to give in. As far as I was concerned, Pete could have ended our conversation at that point. But I had no such luck.

"Y'know," he continued with a note of remorse in his voice, "I didn't spend much time with my kids either. And, no surprise, Bruce, they soon didn't want to spend time with me when they grew older. They didn't want to go fishing. They didn't want to play ball. They had their own friends and their own lives. They just weren't interested anymore. My time with them had gone." Tears formed in his eyes. He seemed deeply pained.

His words forced me to rethink my previous conversation with my wife, my selfish attitude, and how indifferently I had spent last week with *my* children.

To do something difficult as Pete had done—and do it with a good attitude and not in an obligatory way—is a tremendous act of self-denial. When we do something for the good of another person, it is an act of love—the kind of love that is sacrificial, not just a feeling. It is a love that puts *me* second and the *other* first. In that moment we suspend our heart's desire for the heart's desire of the other.

The kind of love I'm describing is difficult and contradicts the trends of our culture. It is a love that revolts against the spoiled child in each of us—that foot-stamping or sulking child who insists things go his or her way.

We all know that it is easy to put on a mask of faith and make an appearance of really living the Christian life. We show up at church, put our dollar in the gold offering plate, and conduct ourselves in a moral manner. We even sit on a few boards that promote good works in the community. It's easy to appear Christian. But there is a significant difference between demonstrating external signs of Christian faith through our public behavior and being truly loving in a Christian way. Too often we *call* ourselves Christian yet live quite selfishly and love meagerly.

Perhaps that's why the apostle Paul wrote to the Corinthians that believers could speak in tongues, share prophetic words, have faith, and give sacrificially to the poor and still lack love. Love, according to Paul, goes beyond our outward behaviors and visible signs of piety. Love must be an internalized attitude that moves us beyond certain instinctive "me first" codes of conduct.

I wonder if Paul penned those words because he had discovered what it meant to live righteously. Of course, before he met Jesus on the road to Damascus, he knew how to live by the law. He knew better than most that a person could be filled with holy vigor and yet lack the ability to be truly loving. But then, gloriously, Paul was changed. Then he was able to say with conviction that true Christian love is modeled in the actions and nature of Jesus. That is, in fact, where love begins.

Then Paul stunningly wrote of Jesus that "though he was God, he did not demand and cling to his rights as God. He made himself nothing; he took the humble position of a slave and appeared in human form" (Phil. 2:6–7 NLT). For the Christian, then, love begins with Jesus. In Jesus we see the model for *emptying* the self. He relinquished his power, his prestige, his personal agenda, his rights, and his place in the universe. Jesus voluntarily became the servant!

Well, then, with Jesus as our starting point, the other challenges that Paul gave the Philippians—and us—become more attainable. He wrote, "Don't be selfish; don't live to make a good impression on others. Be humble, thinking of others as better than yourself. Don't think only about your own affairs, but be interested in others, too, and what they are doing" (Phil. 2:3–4 NLT).

As I have watched the marriages of friends and associates crumble and have watched children grow up unsupervised, unloved, and with little parental involvement, I am eager to find answers to our growing societal crises. And yet I think my carpenter discovered one simple but profound answer to our complex problems. For him it was his willingness to put aside his agenda and go to the beach. Ironically, for most of us going to the beach would be no sacrifice at all. But Pete did the thing that he hated to do because he chose to demonstrate, to live out, his love for his wife.

After a few mistakes along the road, Pete was discovering what it means to be truly loving. I am too.

The Petes of the world remind me of the true essence of love. Of course, I naturally want to love on my terms—to love in ways that fulfill my needs, wants, and desires. But this is a self-serving kind of love. When was the last time you sacrificed your own interests for the interests of another?

A Sacramental Barbie Doll

Love measures our stature: the more we love, the bigger we are. There is no smaller package in all the world than that of a man all wrapped up in himself.

William Sloan Coffin

On a cold January day my wife, Pam, garbed in her signature torn blue-jean overalls with a scarf holding her hair, guided her dented Jeep up a circular cobblestone driveway and parked it at the front door of Mrs. Roberta Gary's magnificent residence.

Mrs. Roberta Gary had *everything*: a million-dollar home in an exclusive community, with each room exquisitely decorated; a high-profile career, which demanded a wardrobe from Neiman Marcus; and two luxury cars in the garage.

She had no needs. What she did have was confidence, maintained by elegance, sophistication, and glamour. She radiated a mature self-assurance.

Pam rang the doorbell.

I would like to say that my wife had a deep, intimate relationship with the owner of this home, but no, she only knew her casually. Their paths had crossed at a few meetings, and they had a few common acquaintances. But to say they really knew each other would have been an overstatement.

The front door opened.

"Hi!" Pam said enthusiastically. "I brought you some thing."

Mrs. Gary, a little perplexed by the whole situation and a little unsure of who was on the other side of the glass storm door, cautiously unlatched the door and took the package my wife was extending. "Uh . . . thanks," she responded, seemingly surprised by having someone come unheralded to her door on *a Saturday*!

"You're welcome," Pam smiled, not knowing if Mrs. Gary even recognized her. "I saw this in a store," she continued, "and thought of you. I just felt you *had to have it*."

My wife waved, turned, and walked back to her car.

When Pam returned home she excitedly told me what she had done. "While window-shopping at a toy store, I came across a Grace Kelly Barbie doll. Something sparked my imagination, and I immediately connected the doll with Mrs. Gary—it just *looked like her*. I had to give it to Mrs. Gary. I bought the doll and dropped it at her house on the way home."

"Are you nuts?" I launched with barbs in my voice. "You dropped a Grace Kelly Barbie doll off at Mrs. Gary's?" I was getting hot. My voice was getting louder. "What would Mrs. Gary possibly want with a doll? She's got everything anybody could ever want! She could *buy* the doll factory." I couldn't believe what my wife had just done.

"How much did it cost?" I inquired.

When she told me that the doll had cost nineteen dollars, I lost it. *What a waste of our family resources.*

Sure, Pam was notorious for her spontaneity. But this was too much! Mrs. Gary would think we were crazy! I mean, who gives a Barbie doll to someone who can afford to buy anything she desires—especially to a very elegant middle-aged woman? My pride was kicking into overdrive. My common sense had been assaulted. I wanted to call and apologize. Mrs. Gary was someone whose respect I wanted.

The phone rang. "This is Roberta, Bruce. May I speak to your wife?" I was stunned. Without a word I thrust the phone at Pam and left.

A normally poised Mrs. Gary told Pam how deeply she was moved by the gift. "That was the first doll I've ever been given in my life. My family was too poor when I was growing up for them to give those kinds of gifts. We emigrated from Eastern Europe when I was a little girl. We had nothing. I've just sat here and looked at her for the past hour. Thank you. Thank you for your creative thoughtfulness." For the next ten minutes, the two women talked and shared. The gift had opened a door. The gift had touched a deep inner chord.

Needless to say, when my wife hung up the phone, she had a smile from ear to ear. I don't know if she was happier about Mrs. Gary's response or the fact that my great commonsense, thrifty approach to life had been put into check. Either way, she had, she said, given a gift that touched a heart. And, to my increasing surprise, over the next three days I was acutely reminded of the gift's impact—there were two more phone calls followed by a two-page letter on gold-embossed personalized stationery!

Pam's act of love reminds me of the bishop's words about *loving wastefully*. That phrase has always stuck with me. Yet it has been much harder for me to implement than to remember. It's easy to love cautiously. It's easy to show expressions of love that are safe and kept within restrained boundaries. But *loving wastefully* always involves risk—there's the risk that the love might be rejected, the risk that the love might not be reciprocated, and the risk that the loving deed might, in fact, *be wasted*.

Yet is it not in *loving wastefully* that we display the inexhaustible love of God? Is it not in these spontaneous, risky acts of love that people are touched and doors are opened?

Remember the woman who used an extravagant perfume to wash Christ's feet—an inappropriate waste in the eyes of some. And yet that woman's act of love has been preserved for over two thousand years as an example of real devotion and spontaneous giving.

I'm not a very impulsive person. I think things through, keep my cards close to the chest, and try to do the practical thing. That day my wife's creative thoughtfulness reminded me that sometimes one *just has to act*, even if it seems a little foolish and a little wasteful—and much, much too spontaneous.

Love should not always be calculated, practical, and measured. Sometimes I find myself analyzing a situation and asking myself, "Is it worth wasting my efforts on this person?" "Is this person going to appreciate my help?" "Is this a good 'investment' of my time and resources?" Sure, we are called to be good stewards with our resources, but we need to be careful that a person's "value" does not drive our ability to love. Fortunately, Jesus chose to model a new way of loving. He dispensed his love freely—to the poor, to the broken, to the little people of his world. Pray that God will begin to liberate your heart to love this way.

> Lord,
> We desire to be wasteful lovers.
> We desire to love lavishly and exorbitantly—
> in ways that transcend social, political, and geographical barriers.
> And yet we meet resistance within ourselves.
> Voices of practicality diminish our love.
> Wounds from our past instruct us to use caution.
> Our culture calls us fools.
> Heal us so we can love more completely.
> Grant us courage to increase the limits of our love.
> Amen.

4

GRATITUDE NOTICED

Was none of them found to return and give praise to God?

Luke 17:18 NRSV

A steaming dinner was served on fine bone china. I was surprised, impressed, and starved. I looked to the other guests to see if it was appropriate to begin eating, but no one had lifted a fork.

Our host stood in the middle of the room. "Please bow your heads," the small, professorial man with bifocals began in a tone of reverential authority. "Lord, thank you for this culinary masterpiece. It is a beautiful piece of art. We are grateful for your gift." He paused. Did I hear right? Did he call this meal *art*? I was surprised. I just wanted to indulge, and he was turning my dinner into a Rembrandt. Get serious. We waited. Were we supposed to be reflecting, or was he having a senior moment? I was about to reach for my fork . . . "And Lord, we pray for the immigrant laborers who picked the beans. We know they often encounter injustice, low wages, and difficult working conditions. We also pray for justice. As well, we pray for their families and the provision of their life's basic necessities. We also pray for those who advocate on their behalf and fight for their rights." My mood sank; this was not going to be an instant grace.

"We pray also for those truck drivers who drive our freeways to deliver our food, often away from their families for days on end. And we pray for those who labor in the potato fields under the hot sun, day after day. May they experience your grace in the midst of their monotonous, backbreaking work. We thank you for their sacrifice. And," he went on without a breath, "for those who have cooked this meal and will wash our dishes, we are grateful. We are grateful, as well, that they have given us the gift of time so that we may engage in exercises of the mind and spirit. We thank you for releasing us from the burden of just eking out a living. This is a privilege." My mind was screaming, *Amen, amen, amen!*

"And now . . . let us enjoy this food that has come to us from so many hands and over so many miles. May we savor it. May we delight in its every morsel. And may our company as well be as delicious as the food before us." He paused, then quietly said, "Amen."

Silence. Slowly the heads rose and eyes opened, looking a little tentative and stunned. We had just been jolted into recognizing the miracle of our meal.

I have heard many prayers in my day. Some prayers, in formal tones, have pontificated the virtues of God; others have been intentionally poetic, as if God were partial to iambic pentameter. Others have had political overtones, as they gloriously acknowledged people of rank and importance in the room. But in all my years of listening to public prayers, I had never heard a prayer that called me to ponder and be grateful for all the people involved in getting the food to my plate.

As I looked at the roasted yams, I had a whole new appreciation for their presence. Now I tried to savor their texture and taste. I tried to eat them in a spirit of gratitude. The prayer had jolted me out of my myopic vision—the self-centered greediness that is so easy to slip into, believing that everything in the world is there for me—into a place of considering others' lives and sacrifices. That prayer called me to take notice of what I so often take for granted—the gift of food. That prayer called me to step outside myself, suspend the impulse of hunger, and engage in a moment that would move me closer to what God hopes for me.

NOTICING GRATITUDE

The Gospel writer Luke recorded a fascinating story that suggests Jesus's interest in and affirmation of the practice of gratitude. Luke's stark narrative places us outside a Jewish village in the region of Galilee. In his story is a ragtag group of roaming men and women with the dread disease of leprosy—a cluster of outcasts traveling together in an effort to avoid contact with the general population. Leprosy is a hideous infectious disease that attacks nerve endings and slowly erodes body parts. In Bible times those afflicted were to be avoided by everyone at all costs, for to come in contact with a leper in that era meant potential physical contamination as well as social and religious isolation. So the lepers of Luke's story were behaving according to their prescribed social status. They stayed away from populated areas. When the lepers encountered Jesus, Luke wrote, "keeping their distance, they called out" (Luke 17:12–13 NRSV). They knew their place. But then the story takes an interesting turn. Nine of the lepers appear to be Jewish, while one is of Samaritan descent. Why is that important?

To understand the impact of this oddity, it is critical to understand the history between the two groups of people, Samaritans and Jews. Samaria (the region where we assume the Samaritan leper originated) was in the northern part of

Israel, generally the area that surrounded the city of Samaria, the capital of the northern kingdom. It was a territory within the borders of Israel, housing a segregated portion of the country's population. Samaritans were negative toward Jews, and the Jews returned the favor. The tension had its roots in a few historical situations. For instance, in the years AD 6–9, the Samaritans desecrated the temple in Jerusalem. The act was reciprocated by the Jewish leaders. In their eyes Samaritans were half-breeds. Because of this dynamic, marriage and sexual contact between the two groups were forbidden. Even their holy places were segregated. For the Samaritan, the place of prayer and sacrifice was Mount Gerizim; for the Jews the holy place was Jerusalem. So, in turn, the Jews thought the Samaritans' temple lacked legitimacy because it was staffed by "renegade priests from Jerusalem."[1]

So why is a Samaritan leper in our group of Jewish lepers? Some scholars believe that since Galilean Jewish lepers had to avoid Jewish villages and Samaritan lepers had to avoid Samaritan villages, both groups of lepers ended up wandering the countryside together. The differences of ethnicity did not matter when neither group had a place to call home. Historical rivalries can be put aside when people are ostracized from the groups that have provided their identity. They can develop a sense of solidarity, much like the solidarity we find in oppressed groups today. And in this particular story, a Samaritan found comradeship with his fellow sufferers.

The roaming outcasts shouted to Jesus, begging for mercy and healing. Surprisingly, the first words Jesus shouted were, "Go and show yourselves to the priests!" Nothing was said directly about healing by Jesus. But Jesus's command was an authoritative command, and that band of dispossessed people began to move in the direction of those who had the power to invite them back into the community—the priests, who upheld the standards of "cleanliness" within the culture. (According to the religious laws of the day, the priest had the exclusive authority to deem people "clean"

or "unclean." Those who were clean could fully participate in the religious and social life of the community. Those
who were unclean were not so fortunate. The custom was
an important part of the community's public health and a
protection from that dread communicable disease that had
no cure at that time.)

Luke continues: "And as they went, they were made clean"
(17:14 NRSV). Jesus had acknowledged the legitimacy of
the religious system of his day. Although he did challenge
the system many times, in this case Jesus affirmed that a
blessing from the priest was the best way for the outcasts to
reintegrate themselves into communal life. Note that Jesus
used the word *priests*, plural, thus acknowledging that the
Samaritan leper would need to go to a different priest than
the Jewish lepers would. It was likely that the Samaritan
would find a priest and offer his sacrifice at Mount Gerizim,
whereas the Jewish lepers would have to go to Jerusalem.
The lepers had to go in different directions. They would
travel separately.

The next section of the story points us to something of
note: "Then one of them," claimed Luke, "when he saw that
he was healed, turned back" (17:15 NRSV). Since it was the
priest who pronounced people clean, a visit to the priest was
absolutely essential for reentering the community. It was
the "visa" that allowed one to roam the streets, shop at the
market, and reunite with one's family. No longer would the
individual need to live on the outskirts of the villages. No
longer would the individual need to worship from behind a
veil, separated from the other worshipers. No longer would
the individual be alienated from public places! Now that's
a great gift.

Yet that Samaritan leper, eager for social reintegration,
headed *back to Jesus*. That was a radical move, a defiant
move.

Fortunately, the Samaritan recognized a force at work
that was greater than the administrative function of a priest.

63

The Samaritan leper had experienced something that the custodians of the religious system could never offer. He had encountered something new and alive—a power and presence that transcended anything the old system could provide. Consequently, there was only one response for the Samaritan. He chose gratitude.

In so doing, the Samaritan expressed his gratitude in three ways. He publicly praised God: "He . . . came back, praising God in a loud voice" (17:15). He physically showed humility by bowing down to Jesus: "He threw himself at Jesus' feet" (v. 16). And he thanked Jesus verbally: "and thanked him" (v. 16). That response of gratitude was what separated the Samaritan leper from the other nine and caught Jesus's attention. "Were not ten made clean?" Jesus sarcastically commented to the onlookers. "The other nine, where are they? Was none of them found to return and give praise to God except *this foreigner*?" (vv. 17–18 NRSV, emphasis added). We can assume that the other nine were racing off to Jerusalem to receive their blessing from the priest. The Samaritan—the foreigner, who in the eyes of Luke's readers should have been the least likely to return and show thanks—was recognized by Jesus for stopping to express thanks for the miracle he had experienced. For his turning back to Jesus—a counterintuitive act of expressing gratitude—Jesus endorsed the behavior of the Samaritan by giving him the ultimate affirmation, "your faith has made you well" (v. 19).

Why did Jesus say, "your faith has made you well," implying that the leper had contributed in some way to his own wellness?[2] Scholars make an important distinction between the ideas of being *healed* and being *cured*.[3] Healing is a physical phenomenon. But just because a person is healed does not mean that he is whole and well. A doctor may heal my arm from a bad break but cannot provide me with a sense of peace and purpose. There is much more to *wellness*.

Wasn't it the Samaritan's willingness to acknowledge God as the healer that separated him from the other nine lepers?

The Samaritan chose gratitude rather than social acceptance. In so doing he transcended the logical (going to the priest) and the emotional (the excitement of the moment) and saw the bigger picture of God's presence in the world. That made him different, an example of what it means to move in the direction of becoming a whole person. A living God, not a religious system, had become the priority in his life. His faith, as expressed through his act of gratitude to God, makes him *well*—not just healed. And Jesus also calls *us* today to notice and ponder the radical activity of this nameless man.

CONTEMPLATING GRATITUDE

Gratitude may be a counterintuitive and countercultural act, especially for us in our possessive, materialistic world. Basic provisions can be quickly forgotten without pausing to acknowledge the miracle of their origin. Contemporary American expectations of what we deserve are off the charts compared to most of the world. Being grateful for a five-year-old computer, a ten-year-old car, penicillin, heat in our home, cool drinks from the refrigerator, or air-conditioning on a hot, muggy day is not generally part of our daily routine. They're basic necessities. Right?

In the midst of difficulties and suffering, finding reasons to be grateful can be extremely difficult. If a loved one is diagnosed with a terminal disease, our response too often is to get angry and complain, not to find a way to look for the good in the midst of the tragedy. If we find ourselves running low on money, our tendency is to whine about how little we possess, not to give thanks for what we do have. If we lose a job, we easily complain; we have difficulty seeing it as an opportunity to start an exciting new career. Being grateful is difficult work. Practicing gratitude can work against our natural instincts.

The late Catholic writer Henri Nouwen spoke insightfully to this truth. He believed that gratitude is *a discipline*.

Gratitude is not something that comes naturally or easily to human beings. It takes intentional effort. "The choice for gratitude rarely comes without some real effort," wrote Nouwen. "But each time I make it, the next choice is a little easier, a little freer, and a little less self-conscious. Because every gift I acknowledge reveals another and another until, finally, even the most normal, obvious and seemingly mundane event or encounter proves to be filled with grace."[4] Making a *choice for* gratitude implies an intentional component to this activity. If Nouwen is right, we are not naturally grateful people. Thus it is important to seek to cultivate a spirit of gratitude. A spirit of gratitude moves us, like the Samaritan leper, closer to wholeness and well-being.

Social philosopher Stephen Carter believes that the lack of willingness to be grateful on the part of so many people is one of the significant cultural problems of our day. When commenting on Gregg Easterbrook's book *The Progress Paradox: How Life Gets Better While People Feel Worse*, Carter draws on Easterbrook's idea. Easterbrook comments, "If the Western world has known a Golden Age, it is right here, right now." Carter then asks the million-dollar question: "Why, then, are people unhappy?"[5] Easterbrook answers by claiming that there is a disconnect between prosperity and happiness: "We need to stop being quite so self-interested, and spend more time on simple gratitude for the remarkable situation in which we find ourselves."[6]

Okay, then how do we "stop being quite so self-interested, and spend more time on simple gratitude"? Easterbrook suggests that it starts by being grateful to God for having *created us*. He also suggests we joyously express gratitude to our families and others who have fought for what we now enjoy. "Failing to feel grateful to those who came before is such a corrosive notion, it must account at some level for part of our bad feelings about the present. The solution—a rebirth of thankfulness—is in our self-interest."[7]

Easterbrook reminds us of Cicero's words, "Gratitude is not only the greatest of virtues, but the parent of all others." And he believes that many of our societal woes would diminish if people began to incorporate this discipline into their lives. Instead of chasing the elusive dream that money and possessions can create happiness, we should begin to look at what we *have* with fresh eyes and a grateful heart.

Like Jesus, we must begin to notice and express gratitude in our everyday lives. As we notice gratitude in the actions of those around us, we should find ourselves drawn to choose the same path for ourselves. And, as Nouwen believes, when we open ourselves to gratitude, we will become increasingly grateful for the most mundane things in our lives—ultimately realizing that there is nothing mundane or boring or unworthy of our attention and praise.

STORIES OF GRATITUDE NOTICED

We all need to be mentored by the example of genuinely grateful people. Paradoxically, the people who often exhibit the deepest expressions of gratitude are those who have experienced life's greatest trials and hardships. These saints rise above their circumstances and embody this virtue of gratitude. I have noticed a few people who have exercised gratitude, and their stories follow. I hope you will begin to notice people in your midst who buck the trends of self-centeredness and practice the discipline of gratitude.

Gratitude on a Greyhound

Books and articles have been important in my search for God, but it has been the interruptions to my everyday life that have most revealed to me the divine mystery of which I am a part.

Henri Nouwen

At 9:05 a.m. I was at the ticket counter of the crowded Greyhound bus station. In fifteen minutes I would be cruising down the turnpike toward Virginia's Blue Ridge Mountains. I was off to a relaxed Christmas holiday at a snowy retreat with my family. I had purchased my ticket a week in advance, so I had little worry that the growing mobs of passengers would get in the way of my securing a seat.

It was Christmas Eve, so warm, nostalgic visions were dancing in my head, especially since my family had left four days earlier to enjoy a few extra days of merriment. Now that my work was done, I could catch up with them, and I had a suitcase filled with presents. The idea of strolling off a bus in a sleepy mountain town to be picked up by my wife and eager children had a sentimental quality that made the idea of a seven-hour bus ride almost bearable.

"We've got seven seats," called the driver when he opened the door of the silver bus. I counted the people ahead of me. Seven . . . eight . . . ten?

"But I purchased my ticket a week ago," I protested to the disinterested driver. "Doesn't that guarantee me a seat?"

"Sorry, sir," he said with annoying indifference. "First come, first served."

"But . . . but," I stammered, "I thought. . . ."

"Read the ticket, sir!" he barked, apparently having been asked the same question a hundred times that day.

As the seventh person disappeared up the bus stairs, I could see his smug smile through the tinted glass. It was probably not even directed at me, but I was steamed. All the passengers were going home for great Christmas celebrations, but not me. I would be eating a sandwich of tuna on stale bread—by myself.

Then, surprisingly, the driver yelled, "We've got room for three more! Come on, let's move, we wanna keep our schedule." Wow! A miracle. Two people preceded me onto the bus. With delight I handed my ticket to the driver and surrendered my bags at the luggage bin. I bolted up the stairwell to claim the last seat.

As I walked the aisle of the crowded bus, trying not to bump anyone with my bulging briefcase, I was perplexed that all the seats were filled. What was going on here? I blinked my eyes, scanning the two rows. *Not a single seat*, just shoulder-to-shoulder indifferent people. This couldn't be true. There was nothing—not even someone trying to sneak extra room for a bag or jacket. I turned and slowly walked back toward the front.

"Somebody was probably in the toilet," grumped the driver. "Sorry, but you'll have to get off." All forty-eight pairs of eyes were riveted on my slumping body as I inched toward the door. They wanted to be on their way.

"Poor child," whispered an elderly woman to her companion. "Guess he ain't gettin' home for Christmas."

My bags were there to greet me as I stumbled onto the landing. The bus pulled out, leaving me in a cloud of diesel fumes. Any nostalgic visions of being home for the holidays evaporated. I dragged my luggage back to the service counter and curtly asked the agent, "Any other buses running to Virginia today?"

She stared at her computer—forever. "Well, you may just be lucky. There's something to Washington in about twenty minutes. You can transfer there and get close to where you'll be goin'." Things were looking up.

Thirty minutes later I boarded the bus to Washington, just hoping and praying there'd be a connection to my destination. Strangely, there were only seven people on the bus, a welcome relief for the emotional state in which I found myself. I needed space to regroup—to take a few deep breaths and convince myself that my pouting was not the best of Christmas moods. But I was in my humbug mode.

I sat down, closed my eyes, and mentally began to plan the next leg of the trip. If there are no connections to the mountains, what will I do? Rent a car? Hitchhike? On Christmas Eve? Probably not. I tried to find solace in the fact that wheels were rolling under me and *I was heading south*. Things will work out, I told myself. The three hours of peace and tranquility will be a balm to the soul.

Then I heard it. At first I tried to block it out, deny it, pretend *it was not happening*. But it persisted, and it wasn't the angels announcing the nativity. I opened my eyes a sliver and tilted my head to the right. In the seat directly across the aisle from me—why, when there were forty-one empty seats?—sat an elderly woman . . . *talking* to herself.

I closed my eyes tight and felt the frustration slowly filtering back into my bloodstream. Would she talk the whole way? Would she ever let up? She had invaded my space. My time to meditate and relax was gone. *Why me?*

Then I heard it—what I had failed to hear earlier. She wasn't talking. She was praying. "Bless you, God. Thank you, Lord. I thank you for your love. You're wonderful. Thank you for your goodness. For health. For provision. Thank you. Thank you!"

For the next twenty minutes I just listened as the woman thanked God in sincerity and humility. As she prayed and sang, it began to dawn on me that I had done more than *literally* miss the bus. Obviously the woman across the aisle, well, *she* was ready for Christmas. She was meeting the Savior—embracing the Christ child in an act of rapturous devotion. By contrast, in my attempts to arrive *on time for* Christmas, I was missing the moment to *be with* Christmas in my deepest self.

But then, on Christmas Eve, in row number 8, seat A, I was mysteriously at the manger with the praises and prayers of an anonymous woman. Like a shepherd of old whose starry solitude was divinely interrupted for a call to a stable, *my* silence was being shattered by the divine incantations of another—angelic utterances that led me to the place I needed to visit.

70

I made it to Virginia and the warm embraces of my family that evening. But that year Christmas, the real Christmas, was on a Greyhound bus.

Do you ever make it a point to just thank God? I find it too easy to only request the things I want and need. Try thanking God for the little things that you take for granted. This is how the discipline of gratitude takes root in our lives.

Gratitude, God, and Lawn Mowers

To lift up the hands in prayer gives God glory, but a man with a dungfork in his hand, a woman with a slop pail, give him glory too. He is so great that all things give him glory if you mean they should. So then my brethren, live.

Gerard Manley Hopkins

I didn't need another phone interruption at that moment, but my secretary insisted. Reluctantly I said, "Yes!" Then added a softer, "May I help you?"

"My name is Jack Harvey. I was wondering if you could use any volunteer help at the ministry. I've been laid off from my job."

Getting calls from people who want to volunteer is not unusual. But sadly I'd discovered that many do not have the skills nor take the time to follow through on their intentions. I asked suspiciously, "What'd you have in mind?"

"Well, I can do just about anything," came the eager reply. I was instantly wary. "You know," he continued confidently, "I can fix vans, cut lawns, clean bathrooms."

Say, this was beginning to sound pretty good. And besides, I had just laid off my maintenance man because of budget cuts, and really, the lawns around our buildings were beginning to look like a South Dakota hay field. And yes, some of the doors of our well-used buildings were falling off their hinges. We really needed help.

"How 'bout tomorrow morning? You can meet our operations director," I said, trying not to sound too desperate.

By ten the next morning the lawn mower, with its high-pitched whine, was churning through six-inch-high grass. It was a welcome sound as our new volunteer huffed his way up and down the grass with a smile on his sweaty face.

On my way to lunch, I decided to thank *my new friend* for his morning efforts.

"Jack," I yelled, trying to drown out the screaming Briggs and Stratton engine. "Got a minute?" He nodded and geared the mower down to a muffled idle. His shirt was like a soaked sponge dotted with grass shavings. "Thanks for being so generous with your time," I said with a smile. "I *really* appreciate your great help."

Before I could heap on more platitudes, he interrupted and looked into my eyes. "God gave me this time as *a gift*. I just want to use it to bless others."

With that, my new volunteer revved up the mower and continued to slice through the grass.

As I headed off to my car, I reflected on Jack's statement. Instead of being bitter about losing his job, stressed about finding a new job, or anxious about his loss of income, this young man had decided to view his time *as a gift to be shared*. He viewed his current circumstances as part of a larger drama—a drama that was being directed by God.

Recently my staff was challenged to look at events, circumstances, and situations from God's perspective. We all realized that it was a somewhat presumptuous undertaking—the idea that we could learn to see things from God's perspective. But was this not the continual challenge of the Christian? Could we begin to put on a God-type lens and thus see events and circumstances in a new light? Rather than viewing unfortunate events as a curse or punishment, could we begin to look for the gift or blessing in such events?

The answer was yes. But it was not easy. And certainly we didn't want to offer as a solution some kind of escapist religion that called us to deny present realities. But we wondered *how we would be changed* when we asked ourselves: "If I view my present misfortune as a gift, how will I respond differently? Can I use the negative situation as a gift for others? Can I use this present circumstance to learn a valuable lesson?" I believe our answers to those questions began to make a difference—both in our lives and in the lives of others.

Periodically UrbanPromise, the inner-city ministry I direct, is in financial difficulty. My natural response, too frequently, is to look at those situations negatively. I wonder, Why is God allowing this to happen? Doesn't God care about the children of this city? What have I done wrong? My questions lean toward the negative and certainly do not reflect the belief that difficult times can be a gift.

However, as I view my troublesome realities as a gift, I learn new lessons: I become less anxious, less stressed. Thus I pray more and become attentive to God's provisions. I find myself taking fewer things for granted. When I view my present reality as a gift from God, resentment and anger can evaporate. Consequently, I discover things I never could have discovered had I not been placed in the difficult situation.

Perhaps this principle is why the imprisoned apostle Paul wrote to the church of Philippi in such an encouraging manner. Rather than viewing his trial and incarceration as unfair—or an example of a lack of God's faithfulness—he saw the presence of God *in and through* the event. He claimed, "What has happened to me has actually helped to spread the gospel" (Phil. 1:12 NRSV). Paul's ability to look at situations from God's perspective ultimately became his gift to the other believers at Philippi. He showed those followers of Jesus how to become more confident and speak with greater boldness without fear (1:14). Paul's directives, happily, are still true for us.

For months my new volunteer continued to bless our community with his gifts of time, muscle, and a joyous spirit. And because he viewed his circumstances as a gift, we received a gift as well.

The older I grow, the more amazed I become at people who can experience the most difficult of circumstances and still find a reason to be grateful. People who develop this ability are usually those who can turn horrible situations into experiences where good things can be birthed. Do you know anyone like Jack who is able to express gratitude in the midst of hardship? How can this attitude impact you?

Subversive Gratitude

The best way to show our gratitude to God and the people is to accept everything with joy. A joyful heart is the inevitable result of a heart burning with love.

Mother Teresa

Dwight went to his doctor to have an MRI. My friend had complained about back pains for a number of months and finally decided to get a checkup. He was the kind of guy who was concerned that he wouldn't be able to play golf.

After the first test, the doctor was concerned, so he ran additional tests. Then the doctor rather straightforwardly told Dwight that he had bone cancer. Dwight was shell-shocked. *Surely this is a bad dream*, he thought. Within moments this healthy thirty-eight-year-old man changed from someone concerned about his golf swing to someone confronting the reality of his own death. His world and his life were suddenly upside down.

Although he was overwhelmed by the news, his diagnosis did not sink in until after the first round of chemotherapy. Dwight, like so many with a cancer diagnosis, was in a stage of denial. But one night as Dwight lay in bed, he lifted his head and found chunks of hair. He ran his hands through his once-thick black hair, and more fell out. He called his wife and showed her what was happening. They held each other and began to cry. Now they would have to face the reality.

It's sobering when the life of someone my own age, someone I care about, takes a dramatic turn for the worse. It quickly puts things in perspective, causing me to reflect and evaluate—to re-assess priorities. Things that once seemed important—like who would win the NBA playoffs, or what the interest rates would be tomorrow, or whether rain would ruin travel plans—become irrelevant in the face of death. Death has a way of challenging us to look more closely at the things we complain about, fret about, and lose sleep over. When facing our mortality, we have a unique opportunity to reprioritize our lives.

Dwight reminded me of this reality. Yet in the midst of his nausea produced by his chemotherapy and his fear of confronting his mortality at such a young age, Dwight's life surprisingly became a living epistle. His experience reminded me that life is short and we never know when we will be greeted by news that will put us into a tailspin.

But what really intrigued and challenged me in Dwight's battle with cancer was something he wrote during the beginning stages of his treatment. As he wrestled with the "whys" and the "why me," he wrote that he tried to "let joy subvert the situation." And to my surprise and delight, despite all the trauma he has encountered, I have watched him *let joy subvert* the difficult circumstances he has encountered. His counte-nance and attitude have been unbelievable—using his smile and laughter to brighten the lives of his friends. His impact on others has been remarkable. He has maintained a sense of humor and a faith that has encouraged many.

"Let joy subvert the situation!" claimed my thirty-eight-year-old friend with death nipping at his heels and every right to be bitter and angry. Dwight had made a decision: he would let joy rule.

His compelling phrase has stuck with me like a burr under my saddle. His idea that *joy can be subversive* has captured my imagination.

Subversion is a wonderful word. It means to overthrow, to cause the downfall, ruin, or destruction of something. To be subversive is to be engaged in activity that leads toward the destruction of something. When I think of subversive activity, I think of the French underground in the Second World War—men and women who risked their lives to undermine the activity and advancement of the Nazi regime. Or I think of the U.S. civil rights workers of the late 1950s and early 1960s who worked to slowly grind down a racist system that allowed privileges to whites while denying the rights of blacks.

So my friend, wisely and insightfully, is letting joy *overthrow* and *destroy* all the negativity, anger, and bitterness that can be associated with his cancer. He is letting joy *ruin* the potentially devastating effects that such an illness can create.

After thinking about Dwight, I began to think about my own life and asked the question, "Am I letting joy subvert my situations?" As I encounter numerous situations each day I ask, "Am I letting joy subvert, undermine, and destroy the negative situations that I encounter?" When a key employee decides to resign with little notice, do I let joy subvert the situation? When a co-worker does something that hurts me, do I let joy subvert the situation? When anticipated travel plans are cancelled because of inclement weather, do I let joy subvert the situation? Sometimes, even most times, I do not. But those words continue to burn in my heart and mind.

When I read the words of the apostle Paul, I encounter someone who attempted to let joy subvert his situations. Rather than living in bondage to his circumstances—imprisonment, stoning, rejections—Paul decided to rise above his situations and rejoice. He decided to let joy subvert each situation. It seems Paul developed a *habit of mind*—a disciplined response to difficult situations. In 2 Corinthians 4, he wrote:

> We are pressed on every side by troubles, but we are not crushed and broken. We are perplexed, but we don't give

up and quit. We are hunted down, but God never abandons us. We get knocked down, but we get up again and keep going.

verses 8–9 NLT

Therefore we do not lose heart. Though suffering, these bodies of ours constantly share in the death of Jesus so that the life of Jesus may also be seen in our bodies. For the trouble we see will soon be over, but the joys to come will last forever.

verses 16–18 NLT

Paul had a *subversive* way of looking at life and life's trials. He did not let hardship destroy him. He did not let difficult circumstances control him. Paul had a way of letting joy subvert situations that would have turned many people to complaints and bitterness. This same Paul later said to the church of Philippi, "Rejoice in the Lord always. I will say it again: Rejoice!" (Phil. 4:4).

I do not know what the long-term medical prognosis is for my friend Dwight. But I do know that his handling of his severe crisis has spoken to me. His words on *letting joy subvert* will stay close to me.

Embracing Dwight's challenge to become subversive people is difficult. Yet when I meet people like Dwight, I begin to see that it is possible. I also receive the gift of seeing the potential impact this choice can have on others. I find myself asking, "What situations can I let joy subvert this week?"

Grateful for Flying Potatoes

Many things occur between God and man which escape the attention of even those to whom they happen.

Abraham Joshua Heschel

It was 102 degrees. August. The rambunctious boys had just completed another day of summer camp. They were hot, tired, cranky, and aggressive as they slumped aboard the bus. Did I mention it was 102 degrees?

I felt growing apprehension when I saw that some of the boys had smuggled leftover brownies from the cafeteria and had sculpted them into well-rounded golf balls. As soon as I pulled out, the chocolate missiles began ricocheting off the walls of the bus.

Surely our new program director, Dez, would defuse the emerging mayhem. I had seen her in action before. She was good. I had started the bus because I knew she could handle it.

But in minutes the first fight broke out. One of the brownies made contact. Then another. There were accompanying insults, punches, and tears, and the whole busload of energetic kids was in mayhem. In the rearview mirror I could see that Dez was struggling to gain control. I pulled off the road. "Sit down!" we yelled in tandem.

Surprisingly, the boys retreated. It was just too hot for a melee.

But the remainder of the trip was anything but peaceful. Too soon new scuffles broke out, resulting in Dez suspending from camp three of the rougher boys—her action antagonized some of the others.

But we were in the homestretch. *Steady as she goes.*

"Drop me off here, mister," demanded one of the boys with menace in his voice. "Yeah, mister, pull over here," chorused a few more. It was hot—105 now in the bus.

"Sure," I said gladly. The faster I could get them off the bus, the faster I could quell the storm and get back to my air-conditioned office. Sure, I felt a twinge of guilt as I eased the bus toward the curb. But it was hot.

As soon as I braked, one of the younger, newer boys bolted out the door. He was angry and trying to make an impression that he too was tough. "I'm gonna *#$@! *brick* this bus," he screamed as he jumped to the street. His threat meant bricks and stones would be hurled at our semi-invalid bus—windows would be broken, the bus undrivable, and the driver terrified. I shifted into first gear and slammed the gas pedal to the floor.

The first projectile smashed the side of our repainted former school bus; then another and another. I began to panic. One of the last kids on the bus screamed, "He's throwing *potatoes* at us. *Rotten potatoes!*"

Sure enough, potatoes were crashing through the open windows like huge hailstones. As the bus lurched past our attacker, half a sack of rotten potatoes rocketed through the open rear window, pelting the seats and rolling down the aisle. What a stench!

As the wounded bus limped back to headquarters, Dez and I created new discipline procedures that were going to be put into place *tomorrow!* We were angry. Those who needed to be suspended were out of here. Follow-up would be done with parents. That was it. We'd had it! We were defeated.

When I calmed down, I said, "You know, Dez, I can't believe I stopped the bus right in front of a bag of rotten potatoes. Think about it. Of all the street corners in the city, how many are likely to have a bag of decomposing potatoes just *sitting* there? We could search the streets for months and never find twenty-five pounds of potatoes on a curb. Bottles, sure. Stacks of newspapers, definitely. But potatoes? Why would God allow that to happen—have us stop right at that spot?" I was wound up.

As was my habit, I was soon trying to make some kind of *theological* sense out of the pelting of our aging bus and my bruised ego. I was resentful that I was going to have to spend the next couple of hours scraping rotten potatoes off the seats and scrubbing the outside of the bus. Why didn't God intervene in some miraculous way and make our day a little easier?

"You know, Bruce," Dez said with a smile, "that kid said he was going to brick the bus. If he had *bricked* the bus, we would have been in serious trouble—windows would have been broken, kids injured, the whole bus a dented mess." Dez paused, then provided her poignant final line. "Maybe God did intervene. It was God's grace that only potatoes were there—soft, rotten, smelly potatoes."

I chuckled. Dez was right. If I had to choose between a few rotten potatoes coming through my windows versus bricks and stones—potatoes, no contest. Could it be that God's caring grace was in the flying potatoes? No major damage was done. No one was hurt. I should be grateful!

But, you know, I have a skeptical, suspicious side. So now when I drive the streets, I keep looking for bags of rotting potatoes. Interestingly, I haven't found any—yet. There are lots of bricks, stones, and broken beer bottles. But no potatoes.

Perhaps, just perhaps, God's grace sometimes, unsuspectingly, humorously, comes to us disguised as rotten potatoes.

Oh, and by the way, today's temperature is a refreshing 75 degrees.

It is a challenge to see beyond our immediate circumstances, especially when events do not go our way. But I am finding that these are the moments when I need to look for expressions of God's grace and goodness. Oddly enough, these expressions are often hiding, and we just need to open our eyes. I am grateful for people like Dez who can see God's hand in a hailstorm of potatoes.

> Lord,
> We naturally bend toward self-preservation,
> self-exultation,
> and self-centeredness.
> We tend to complain too much.
> We tend to focus on our shortcomings.

Help us to notice those who choose a path of thanks
and joy.
Grant us the discipline to develop an attitude of
gratitude.
Amen.

5

CHILDREN NOTICED

Have you never read, "Out of the mouths of infants and
nursing babies you have prepared praise for yourself"?

Matthew 21:16 NRSV

Why I asked the question, I'm not sure.
But let me go back to 6:30 one Sunday morning. I had driven our rusty fifteen-passenger van to pick up children for church. First there were the twenty kids who needed to be at choir practice by 8:00. Then there were the multiple runs to get kids to the pancake breakfast—which a few faithful volunteers had been preparing since 7:30. Before church at 10:00, seventy-five hungry kids would devour stacks of steaming flapjacks soaked in warm maple syrup and butter.

The aging but proud church had only fifteen elderly members who continued to attend the family church they grew up in. Our infusion of sometimes unruly neighborhood kids was reluctantly tolerated but was a significant attendance boost to the morning service. Few churches in the area could boast of such a high child-to-adult ratio. And 500 percent growth in a changing urban neighborhood was a record that would impress any denominational leader.

After the pancakes had been devoured that particular Sunday, I escorted the children to the sanctuary and got them seated. I had never really noticed before, but on the wall was a wooden sign: ATTENDANCE LAST YEAR, 15. Below that it said ATTENDANCE TODAY, 14. *How odd*, I thought. The first seven rows of the sanctuary were *filled* with happy, whispering kids.

"Mr. Barring?" He was the eighty-year-old head trustee. "I'm a little confused. Why are there only fourteen people on the weekly attendance board? By my count there are ninety-two people in the sanctuary today. Is there some mistake?"

Like I said, why I asked the question, I am not sure. Was my ego getting the best of me? Being up since 6:30, driving through potholed streets, and picking up sleepy kids who were seldom dressed and ready when I pulled up in front of their houses certainly had made me a little edgy. (Well, at least that was my excuse.)

I was somewhat surprised when Mr. Barring whispered in his best Sunday-morning-church voice, "There's been no mistake. *We* don't count *those* children."

Raising my voice slightly, I said, "What do you mean you don't count *those* children?"

"Well," he said matter-of-factly, "they're not *our* children."

If I had not been so angry, I would have burst out laughing. Fifteen graying seniors, trying to prop up the last vestiges of a dying congregation, could not even acknowledge the infusion of life and vitality that had entered their church in the form of beautiful, lively, expressive children. Due to some logic that escaped me, it appeared that neighborhood children were not viewed as full participants, nor counted, in worship. But didn't the failure to acknowledge the children on the aging, mahogany attendance board reflect a feeling of superiority? Obviously the children were invisible guests. Their presence, ideas, and potential contributions to the fading congregation were not to be considered. Could it be that maybe, just maybe, our children weren't counted because they were African American and Latino—invaders in a community that was once all white?

By not counting our children, the congregants missed the great potential the children brought to the fellowship—a potential that Jesus celebrated. He made a point of saying that embedded in the life of each little one is a dimension of God's presence that will enrich, enlighten, and challenge. But this potential was missed by those remaining adults who, I am afraid, were blinded by the same mind-set that blinded the disciples of Jesus—a mind-set that attributed false value to people on the basis of age, gender, and social status. But that dismissive attitude provoked a strong rebuke and challenge from Jesus. Jesus made it very clear that if the disciples were to learn the ways of God, they would need to embrace and *notice* children.

WHY NOTICE CHILDREN?

Children played an important role in the life and teachings of Jesus. This theme is highlighted by the fact that Matthew, Mark, and Luke all recorded Jesus's conflict with his disciples over their apparent misunderstanding of a child's place in his mission. The Gospel writers emphasized that children were more than passive recipients of prayer and blessing from Jesus. Children, for Jesus, were a living metaphor of authentic discipleship.

Mark records Jesus saying of children, "Anyone who doesn't have their kind of faith will never get into the Kingdom of God" (10:15 NLT). According to New Testament scholar Judith Gundry-Volf, this claim is radical because nowhere in Jewish literature are children put forward as models for adults, and in a Greco-Roman setting, comparison with children was highly insulting.[1] Jesus's claim no doubt shocked and jarred his listeners. If *entering* the reign of God is conditional upon *receiving* it as a child, then understanding the implications of Jesus's statement is critical for those who want to live a life that reflects the nature and values of God.

Gundry-Volf helps clarify this statement by claiming that Jesus can be interpreted two ways. "Either Jesus is referring to adults' adopting a *childlike status*—similar to his telling the rich young ruler to exchange his position of privilege by selling all he has and giving the money to the poor (see Mark 10:17–22), or Jesus is referring to emulating some presumed *childlike quality*."[2] Adopting this childlike quality is the probable interpretation of this passage.

But if this is the case, what aspects of childlikeness must *we* emulate? Surely it is not the temper tantrums of a two-year-old nor the self-centeredness of an adolescent. For to romanticize childhood and overlook those aspects that seem antithetical to the teachings of Jesus would lead us astray from Jesus's intent. Thus Gundry-Volf encourages us to read all the child-related passages in the Gospel narratives. And when we do, we discover that the childlike quality that needs to be emulated is the virtue of *humility*. When Jesus talked about becoming *childlike*, it was an illustration for those who were arguing about their greatness or exercising their power and social status as adults. Gundry-Volf adds, "Just as 'little ones' are special objects of divine care and protection, and to despise and mistreat them is to put oneself at cross-purposes with the God of the weak and oppressed and at risk of divine judgment, so also to humble oneself and 'receive' little children, as Jesus does, is to be great in the reign of God."[3] Jesus underscored the importance of humility and equated this kind of humility with greatness.

Perhaps Jesus was so forthright about humility because a lack of humility restricts one from truly embracing God and those God loves. Humility challenges our illusions that we are the center of the universe. Joan Chittister, who writes so beautifully about Benedictine spirituality, reminds her readers that at the center of Saint Benedict's writings on spirituality is the theme of *humility*. In fact, Saint Benedict believed so strongly in the need for followers of Jesus to embrace humility that he developed twelve steps to help people move toward humility. Chittister writes, "The pride that is the opposite of monastic humility is the desire to be my own God and to control other people and other things. . . . It is pride to want to wrench my world and all the people in it to my ends. It is arrogance to the utmost to insist that other people shape their lives to make mine comfortable. It is arrogance unabashed to think that God must do the same."[4] Jesus did not have any room for arrogance and pride in the new world he was trying to create. When Jesus identified self-serving behavior surfacing in the lives of his disciples, he alerted them to the dangers of it. When Jesus saw dangerous forms of stultifying religion expressed in the lives of the religious leaders, he exposed them and warned his followers. The most eye-catching example of humility that Jesus placed in front of his listeners was children.

But be cautious, for our prideful tendencies do not simply stop because we notice humility in children. For if we adults truly embody the spirit of humility and *receive* children, then we must open ourselves to the fullness of what children can teach—an act that is difficult for us as prideful adults who *know everything*. But according to Jesus, learning from children is critical because children have special links to God. This dynamic is best illustrated in Matthew 21, where Jesus confronts the religious leaders because of their anger toward children who have acknowledged that Jesus is the Son of David. The religious leaders had a difficult time swallowing

87

the truth that those children had a spiritual insight they did not: the children *noticed* the identity of Jesus. The adults did not. By saying, "Have you never read, 'Out of the mouths of infants and nursing babies you have prepared praise for yourself'?" (Matt. 21:16 NRSV), Jesus affirms that children, then and today, speak truthfully about his identity. God has given them insight and has opened their mouths with a holy innocence.

"Children are not mere ignoramuses in terms of spiritual insights in the Gospel tradition," argues Gundry-Volf. "They know Jesus' true identity. They praise him as the Son of David. They have this knowledge from God and not from themselves, and because they do, they are living manifestos to the source of all true knowledge about Christ as from God. Jesus' affirmation of the children's praise of him in this passage is thus an affirmation that children who 'know nothing' can also 'know divine secrets' and believe in him."[5]

Prideful, self-important adults may have difficulty with this rhapsodic affirmation. The idea that children can have insight into spiritual things flies directly in the face of our adult preoccupations and makes us wince, for we glean our spiritual insights from well-trained seminarians with theological degrees who wax eloquent in burnished pulpits. Jesus suggested, on the contrary, that our sources of spiritual revelation should not be limited to those with degrees. Spiritual revelation also comes "out of the mouths of babes." Yes, difficult as it sometimes can be, adults can glean spiritual insight from a child.

Perhaps that is why biblical scholar Jürgen Moltmann writes, "With the beginning of a new life, the hope for the reign of peace and justice is given a new chance. It is important to see children in their own transcendent perspective and so to resist forming them according to the images of our world. Every new life is also a new beginning of hope for a homeland in this unredeemed world."[6] The idea of "seeing children in their own transcendent perspective" is to notice children in ways that affirm their sacred nature and their potential to mentor adults who desire to live closer to the heart of God.

CONTEMPLATING CHILDLIKENESS

"Oh, come on, Jesus!" we cry in protest. "You don't work or play with the same children I work with! You don't spend your day changing diapers, supervising playgrounds, or breaking up fights between selfish little brats who watch too much television and are addicted to video games. Jesus, you have never had a lazy, spoiled fourteen-year-old who does not want to go to school. And get him to do homework? Forget about it!"

For many of us the only thing we notice about children is their self-centeredness and unwillingness to share. The idea of a child offering any kind of spiritual direction or insight is a lofty ideal that sounds wonderful coming from the mouth of a wise spiritual teacher but has little chance of becoming a practical practice. Our stress level is too high, our patience is worn thin. Our lives are busy, and who has the time to really notice the unique and special behaviors of children?

But pause a moment and take a deep breath. Jesus was telling us to *make the effort*. Jesus was saying that along with our Bible readings, our devotional times, and our moments of prayer, children have the potential to break through the ordinary and provide us with living examples of what it means to be *truly great*. So begin to look and in a fresh way welcome the little ones. Take note of the moment—between the screaming and the whining—when you can catch a glimpse of what *childlikeness* is all about. And when you catch glimpses of behavior that show the heart of God, begin the slow, enriching process of implementation.

STORIES OF CHILDLIKENESS NOTICED

Becoming childlike, or humble, is difficult. It can cut against the grain of our personalities and our adult tendencies. Often our need to find approval from our peers or colleagues prevents us from acting in a childlike manner. And yet we see something beautiful in the simple actions of a child. There is something prophetic, at times, in their concrete language and their clear vision of how the world should work. I consider myself blessed to spend much of my time in the midst of children. They have become my teachers and mentors. I trust you will begin to notice children and the lessons they can teach us.

Praying with Henry

Adults need children in their lives to keep their imagination fresh and their hearts young and to make the future a reality for which they are willing to work.

Margaret Mead

Six-foot-tall, handsome, prestigious attorney Lee Harp sat scrunched at a preschool table, knees pressed to his chin, trying to look comfortable. He slowly unwrapped a chicken fillet sandwich. His wispy hair, silver-rimmed bifocals, white shirt, and Windsor-knotted tie spoke of someone who frequented the upscale, trendy bistros of the area for lunch rather than our makeshift cafeteria. He was in the assembly hall of our budding private school. Today Lee Harp would forfeit the crystal glassware, the shrimp Lamaze, the glass of chilled chardonnay, and the strolling violins. Instead, it was chicken on a bun, a Juicy Juice, and the cacophony of screaming children.

This was Mr. Harp's first visit to "Partner Day"—a day that our school sets aside to bring donors and potential donors to have lunch with our students. Because we are a school for low-income urban kids, finding people to create scholarships for our children is a daunting task. Our odds of discovering generous donors increase when we invite prospective philanthropists to have lunch with a child.

Mr. Harp's religious commitments were vague. At one point in his life he had attended church, but he had become disillusioned with its hypocritical politics. Later he tried a nondenominational congregation in an effort to get his obstreperous teen back on track, but the loud, contemporary style of worship drove him away. Church was now a walk with his dog on a Sunday morning, then playing a CD of Handel's *Messiah* while reading the *Times*. He asked, "Just how religious is this school you run here?" revealing his hesitation and reservation about things religious. "This Christian stuff makes me uneasy."

Now everyone was seated, so Lee Harp reached for his sandwich. He was interrupted by the disapproving look of Henry Brown Jr., the fourth grader sitting at his right. Lee pulled his hands—and sandwich—back. "We haven't said grace yet!" rebuked the serious fourth grader in a disarming way. "We always say a prayer before we eat."

It had been years—maybe ten—since Lee Harp had prayed a prayer. The lawyer, who made his living creating spellbinding arguments for juries and judges, wasn't quite sure what to do. Who was supposed to pray in these kinds of situations? The adult? The child?

Fortunately, without hesitation the wide-eyed boy reached across the table, took Mr. Harp's hand, and bowed his head. "Dear God," he began, "thanks for my new friend, Mr. Harp. Thanks for bringing him to me. Thanks for giving us a chance to eat lunch together. Thanks for this wonderful food. We pray that you will bless this day and watch over our families. In Jesus's name, amen."

A tear crept down Mr. Harp's face. It had been a long time since he had heard such a beautiful, sincere prayer of thanksgiving—a prayer prayed with childlike faith and gratitude.

"He prayed with such *ease*," exclaimed the emotional Harp later to some of our staff. "It was like he was just having a conversation with God." Lee could not get over the idea that someone could talk so easily and comfortably with God.

I heard later that Lee Harp, prominent attorney, could not stop telling the story. He told everyone at his law firm, much to the chagrin of his colleagues. Everyone in his family heard the story. Harp became an evangelist, telling the story of this simple act of faith to anyone who would listen. His heart had been touched deeply by Henry's act of innocent devotion to God. And Lee could not keep quiet.

I wonder if Lee Harp represents a growing number of people whose faith has been relegated to the back closets of their lives because they have not seen any authentic expression of faith. Yes, our liturgy speaks truth, but it seldom seems to be embodied in the lives of those who recite it. Hymns promote lofty ideals of love and grace that seldom seem to be realized in the lives of those who sing them. Those in pulpits often exhort people to higher levels of morality, but they too often fall short themselves. In this postmodern world where religious authority is questioned and vilified, people are skeptical.

Eugene Peterson writes, "People are fed up with leaders and friends who talk learnedly and officiously about God but show little evidence of being interested in God. People are fed up with leaders and friends who tell them what to do but show very little interest in who they are."[7] It is this inability to integrate faith and faithlike practice that concerns Peterson.

Peterson goes on to challenge believers to strive toward what he calls "congruence"—the ability to become one with what we believe. Faith, according to Peterson, is not some external set of actions. Rather, belief and actions are supposed to be one. When this oneness happens, our lives have the potential of becoming a powerful testimony to those who stand at a distance with jaded hearts.

Little Henry Brown, unabashed, did what his faith told him to do and did not think about the consequences. Because of his action, an aging, proud man who had all but given up on faith had another glimmer of hope—hope that this "Christian stuff" was real and that talking to God with ease might be a good place to start.

Perhaps this is why Jesus, who was always excited by and comfortable with the children around him, said, "Anyone who will not receive the kingdom of God like a little child will never enter it" (Luke 18:17).

Henry Brown brightens my day every time I pass him in the hallway. Obviously he brightened Mr. Harp's life this past Partner Day. I am trying to figure out what I need to learn from this little guy. Perhaps it is the unrehearsed congruity that he displays between his growing faith and his life—a congruity that I need to continually seek in my own life.

The Unexpected Samaritan

Everybody can be great. Because anybody can serve. You don't have to have a college degree to serve. You don't have to know about Plato and Aristotle to serve. You don't have to know Einstein's Theory of Relativity to serve. You don't have to know the second theory of thermodynamics to serve. You only need a heart full of grace. A soul generated by love.

Dr. Martin Luther King Jr.

Kay Smith was a seventy-eight-year-old white woman. It quickly became evident after talking with her that like too many Americans, this woman—plain and simple—did not like black people. Kay, like so many others who had once lived in the city of Camden, blamed African Americans for everything. It was *their* fault that the city was not the way it used to be. *They* were the problem. If only *they* would leave, the city would somehow return to the glory days when people safely walked the streets, left their doors open, and drank malts at the corner drugstore.

Within a few days of the start of a summer youth program at her nearby Baptist church, it became apparent to Kay that the outreach to children in the neighborhood was certainly going to create conflict with the remaining church congregants. The church had not done anything in the community for the past ten years, and Kay did not like the idea of neighborhood boys and girls invading her sacred space.

As soon as kids were eagerly flocking to the church for our programs, I started getting calls from the trustees concerning things that had happened that day in camp. I was amazed that these men, who lived nowhere near the church, would have the kind of information they had. It was as if they had been there at the church all day, watching every move.

Finally, I realized their source. It was Kay Smith. She lived across the street and watched the church property like a hawk. In the morning she would see the kids run wildly around the parking lot. At lunch she would see an occasional kid pitch his sandwich wrapper on the ground. There was the infrequent bottle smashed and the incessant pounding on the church door. But cussing and wrestling on the front lawn were too much. Each night a call would be made to trustees informing them of all the bad things that had taken place that day. With her steady flow of angry tidbits, we did not think we would make it through the summer. She wanted us out—now! Naturally, she was alarming the congregation.

One especially hot mid-July day, Kay Smith ventured out of her house for a quart of milk. About a block into her journey back home, she began to feel a little dizzy. It wasn't the heat of the day; it was the humidity—one of those breathless East Coast days New Jersey is famous for. Kay began to lose her bearings. She decided that she had better sit down on the curb and rest a little before finishing the journey. She tried to find a shady place.

Our summer program had just been released for the day, and ten-year-old Tiombe came skipping up Westfield Avenue, oblivious to the heat because she had just had the time of her life. Earlier that week she had been learning about the good Samaritan. Flannelgraph lessons had been taught, Scriptures memorized, and skits presented. Tiombe had learned about the man who had gone out of his way to help the wounded man at the side of the road.

Skipping from line to line on the cracked concrete sidewalk, Tiombe saw an old lady sitting on the curb with a sweating carton of milk beside her.

"Can I help you, ma'am?" called the little African American girl. Tiombe waited for the response. Kay didn't say a word. She just sat there looking dazed.

"Can I help you?" pleaded Tiombe a little louder.

This time Kay nodded at the girl but could not answer.

Without hesitating, little Tiombe gently took hold of the fragile woman by the arm and steadily helped her to her feet. With her free hand she grabbed Kay's slippery quart of milk, and she began to slowly help the old woman down Westfield toward her house. Tiombe had seen Ms. Smith many times sitting on her porch and knew just where to go.

Upon arriving on the landing of the white-and-green row house, little Tiombe held out the quart of milk to the frail, swaying woman, gave her a gentle hug, whispered "God bless you," and then skipped off the porch.

A few days after the incident, I received a call in my office. Being unaware of the story, when I heard the voice at the other end of the receiver, I surmised that once again I was in for it. I had a sense our program was about to be over. The program would be shut down. The trustees and the critics had won, and Ms. Smith was calling to gloat over her victory. But to my surprise, the tone was not the same. After a few minutes of unusual friendly chitchat about the weather, Ms. Smith, in her slow, elderly drawl, told me that she thought the program was doing just fine. She was *glad* we were there.

We were allowed to continue the programs, and an elderly woman had been changed! A child had broken through the years of bitterness and racial hatred. Through the actions of a ten-year-old girl, a seventy-eight-year-old woman had been transformed.

I often wonder how many great sermons Kay Smith had heard in her lifetime. She had been going to church all her life. Sunday after Sunday she had heard well-trained pastors preach earnestly about the love of Christ. Year after year she had heard messages preached from Genesis saying that we are all created in the image of God or from the letters of Paul proclaiming that there is "no longer Jew or Gentile, slave or free" in Christ (Gal. 3:28 NLT). And yet somehow the words of that Bible preaching had not penetrated her heart.

But when a ten-year-old girl heard Jesus's story of an unlikely man being moved with compassion for a stranger and this same little girl acted upon what she had heard, it had a powerful impact. Tiombe heard the Jesus story, acted on it quite literally, and touched a heart hardened by years of bitterness.

A child did what all the preachers could not do. Tiombe, a child, was used by God. Her age, her skin color, and her educational background had nothing to do with her capacity to prompt change.

Saint Francis of Assisi once said, "Preach the gospel always. If necessary, use words." And from a child we learn, one more time, that the best sermons are always those when words are embodied in action, presenting an integrated truth that cannot easily be dismissed by argument or reason. In the humility of a child's action, we are given a beautiful image of what life should be when we seek to reflect the heart of God in all we do and say.

One of the beautiful things about watching children is seeing how quickly they can make friends—regardless of skin color and culture. What do I need to learn from Tiombe? I believe I need to embody her willingness to simply act out the teachings of Jesus in daily life. As an adult I find it easy to justify my inactivity. I can often come up with a hundred reasons not to put into practice the teachings of Jesus. But Tiombe challenges me to remember that there is power in the doing.

"I Seen God and Lived"

You keep us looking.
You, the God of all space,
Want us to look in the right and wrong places
For signs of hope
For people who are hopeless,
For visions of a better world that will appear
Among the disappointments of the world we know.
So thank you . . . for the looking time.

Iona Community, Scotland

Ms. Harris called her first-grade class to the front of the room. On cue sixteen eager boys and girls sat cross-legged on the slightly worn, brown, oval rug. They always looked forward to hearing her daily Bible stories. Today's story was from Genesis.

"Did you know that no one has ever seen God?" began the confident teacher as she sat with her Bible opened on her lap. "Moses came closest, but God made Moses turn his back when he was passing by because, children, no one can see God and live."

"I think you're wrong, Ms. Harris. I seen God!" interrupted six-year-old Larry with an unusual note of confidence in his voice. Larry Gaines kept shaking his head in disapproval. Ms. Harris knew that three weeks earlier, Larry's father had died, and since then his behavior had become less predictable. She also knew that she had been caught off guard. Sure, she was used to the children interrupting her

97

lessons, but never did a child say she was wrong about the Bible. After all, she knew the Scriptures were clear.

She continued. "I don't think so, Larry. No one can see God and live. That's what the Bible says."

"But I saw him, Ms. Harris. I did," insisted Larry even more earnestly. "God came to me in a dream."

By this time the other children had begun to giggle. They thought it was just Larry acting up again; he was always funny and clowning around. No one else dared talk to the teacher like he just had. Ms. Harris sensed that there was no chance now of changing Larry's mind. "So, what happened in your dream?" she said encouragingly.

Larry paused for a moment and looked pensively back at his teacher. He was uncharacteristically serious. "God came in the sun and separated the sun in two pieces and then spoke to me." Now Ms. Harris was intrigued. The classroom giggles had subsided as everyone wanted to hear what God had to say to Larry.

"God said, 'I know how badly you want to play with your dad, Larry. But he's playing with *me* now, Larry. We're playing together, and we're having lots of fun.'" Larry paused again. Everyone sensed that he had more to say.

Ms. Harris nodded for him to continue. He said, "And then I smiled, Ms. Harris, because I knowed everything was okay. You can't tell me I didn't see God, 'cause I saw him." A somewhat flustered Ms. Harris scrambled to bring the lesson to an awkward close.

I've yet to find out how Ms. Harris, that excellent though learning teacher, reconciled Larry's revelation with her belief that God cannot be seen. And I'm glad I wasn't teaching the class.

Psychoanalyst Sigmund Freud would have had a field day with little Larry's dream. His analysis probably would have suggested that Larry's dream and "conversation with God" were actually the result of some unresolved, deeply rooted, unconscious longing to see his father—merely a coping mechanism for him to deal with his father's tragic death.

Freud notwithstanding, I would rather look at Larry's dream through the lens of knowing a loving God who displays grace to suffering little boys and provides peace during difficult times.

Scholar and writer James Huston once said that the unique thing about God's love is its *particularity*. Huston emphasized that God's love is infinite in particularity, not quantity. There is a difference, he said.

Yes, we worship a God "whose eye is on the sparrow" and who knows "the number of hairs on our heads." And that is *particular* love. That is an attentive love that notices *individual* people. That is the love of the Good Shepherd who knows when even one sheep is missing.

Has anyone ever seen God and lived? Sure, Larry has. And because of this revelation of grace, I am reminded that God does not love us in just a general sense—God loves each of us in a particular sense. And because of that assurance, I can say with little Larry Gaines, everything will ultimately be okay for those of us with the same faith as a child.

I believe Larry Gaines experienced an act of God in his life. This little boy needed comfort, and God visited him in a dream. The best part of the story was his willingness to share this revelation with his classmates and challenge his teacher. How many glimpses of God's grace do we miss because of our inability to become childlike? How many opportunities do we miss to tell the world of God's particular kind of love because sharing might make us seem foolish?

What about Forgiveness?

In this way we differ from all animals. It is not our capacity to think that makes us different, but our capacity to repent, and to forgive. Only humans can perform that most unnatural act, and by doing so only they can develop relationships that transcend the relentless law of nature.

Aleksandr Solzhenitsyn

Preaching at the Presbyterian church around the block from us is always a challenging experience. It's a hundred-year-old church that sits on the corner of 36th and Merriel Streets in a once-proud town.

Back in its glory days, it was *the* premiere church. Only the best families strolled to church each week from their nearby elegant Victorian homes. That church had a presence in the community. But sadly, things are different now. Over the past thirty years the church members have dwindled to a handful.

I remember the first Sunday I preached there. It was a hot, sultry August morning. The sanctuary windows had been cranked open in a desperate attempt to catch a few wisps of early morning breeze. The meager crowd was restless, and paper fans kept pace with my preaching rhythms. As I was moving toward the climax of my sermon, slowly and grandly building toward a crescendo and a call to action, the congregation was with me. Intruding on that crucial moment, startling us all, came a screeching of tires followed by a tremendous crashing sound. Everyone froze. Then, in the next heartbeat, the parishioners headed out the front doors. I was left speechless. Well, yeah, there *were* three little old ladies in the front pew who didn't move. But what should I do? Should I finish? Should I wait? Should I close with the benediction?

The big surprise was that after ten sweltering, confusing minutes, everyone began to trickle back inside. But the sermon was gone. The mood was broken. So I said the benediction.

But that was an easy day. The next time I was invited to preach, I was greeted by twenty energetic junior highers, all seated in the first six rows on the left side of the sanctuary. "I decided to keep 'em upstairs today," announced Brent, the youth director.

I had anticipated speaking to about fifteen graying adults; my sermon was not geared toward twenty restless kids; my illustrations, frankly, had more of an adult flavor. *That's great*, I thought. *Not only will my message be over the kids' heads, but they'll be bored and restless.* I knew I was in trouble, so I started making mental outline adjustments. Prune from three points to two. Drop the inappropriate illustrations, grab for others. Anything to keep the kids captivated.

I began, "If you come to the altar . . . and there remember your brother has something against you. . . ." I was quoting Jesus from the sixth chapter of Matthew. I talked about forgiveness—the importance of forgiveness and the need to forgive. I had a freedom that really carried me to the points I wanted to make.

The kids sat spellbound through all twelve and a half minutes without making a sound. Not only that, but one of the kids said after the service, "You shoulda preached longer."

But lest I should get feeling too grand, the next day Brent took some of the glow off the worship moment when he relayed to me what had happened *after church*.

He had taken the newly sermonized group of guys to the gym to play a little basketball. While playing, a couple of the kids got in a scuffle. "You fouled me!" screamed one. "No way," retorted the other, enraged. Before Brent could figure out what was happening, he had a real brawl on his hands. And being a little frazzled from having spent a good part of his Sunday with these kids, Brent lost it.

"You're both outta here!" he yelled at the top of his lungs. "Gone! Now! Get your jackets." The two boys, never having seen Brent so angry, quickly headed toward the door.

"Wait a minute!" yelled ten-year-old Pedro. "Wait a minute, *everybody*." He raised his hands as if he were a cop stopping traffic for a presidential motorcade. He summoned the two boys back to the middle of the gym floor.

"What about forgiveness? What about forgiveness, you guys?" He grabbed the two boys, brought them into the middle of the circle, and said, "Ya gotta shake hands. Shake hands, I say. *Shake hands*."

Reluctantly, the two warring boys lifted their hands, put aside their pride, and limply shook hands. "Now say you're sorry. Come on," urged Pedro, "*say it!*" By this time little Pedro was pushing the issue to the edge. Shaking hands was tough enough, but saying "sorry"?

"Sorry," whispered one of the boys. "Sorry," muttered the other. Then Pedro did the unthinkable. He went beyond the edge. He went to the place that no preadolescent boy wants to go. "Now hug each other. Come on. Hug!" came the final request from little Pedro.

Knowing they had no choice, the two boys awkwardly reached out and embraced. It wasn't an intimate hug; it was one of those distant, two pats on the back, semicool hugs. *But they did it.* Pedro then gave a new command: "Let's play ball!"

One person heard the sermon that morning. The message had gone forth, and it had been received. And maybe, just maybe, God needs the literal interpretation of a child to get the message to those who need to hear.

How many great sermons have I heard in my life and forgotten within ten minutes of the final hymn? And yet the real power of a sermon is when we decide to put the message into action. Pedro reminds me of the life-changing implications when we put our faith into practice. It may seem small and insignificant at the time, but we never know the impact over the course of time.

Lord,
It is hard to embrace childlikeness in this competitive
    world.
Humility comes as a challenge for most of us.
And yet we know that there is a sacred quality in
    children.
Open our eyes to embrace the lessons we need to
    learn from your little ones.
Amen.

6

COMPASSION NOTICED

But a Samaritan, who was on a journey, came upon him;
and when he saw him, he felt compassion.

Luke 10:33 NASB

The nineteenth-century Danish philosopher and theologian
Søren Kierkegaard wrote a meditation on the parable
of the good Samaritan. In it Kierkegaard emphasized that
three men walked down a road, just an ordinary road, on
an ordinary day.

His three men had different backgrounds, different profes-
sions, and presumably different social standings. But that was
of little concern to Kierkegaard. Strip away the titles and the
careers and the social standings and he found . . . well . . .
just three men, typical human beings, just like us.

Here's the catch, and I think this was the point Kierkegaard wanted to make: it's not the road we travel; it's how
we travel the road.

Kierkegaard believed that many of us do not fully engage ourselves in our traveled journey. Like the priest and the Levite, we become seduced into thinking about *other* roads—greener pastures, future destinations. The priest of the parable was obviously traveling his road of future priorities or fears—the insistent priestly duties he needed to perform that afternoon without violating the rules and regulations of his religion. The Levite was also traveling another road, a road of better opportunities—perhaps afternoon appointments, potential business deals, and family obligations. Whatever the case, both men were preoccupied and unable to fully engage the road they were traveling that morning. They could not give their full attention to the road and what it asked of them. They did not travel in a way that Jesus affirmed as a way that reflected the heart and nature of God.

But then there was the Samaritan, the *good* Samaritan. He was not oblivious to his road. His heart, his mind, and his will were all present with the rocks and dust and spectacle of the Jerusalem-to-Jericho road. But then, as he rounded the bend in the road, there was the man, obviously beaten by thugs or robbers.

None of the original hearers of Jesus's story would have been shocked if no one had stopped for the beaten man. So Jesus went for the jolt. He used a Samaritan as the story's hero to surprise his Jewish audience. The idea of a Samaritan stopping to help a Jewish man was radical. Samaritans were despised by Jews and looked upon as impure people—just half-breeds. A Samaritan received the same disdain and scorn as a biracial child would have received from a white majority while growing up in the southern United States during the height of segregation. But according to Luke's telling, the Samaritan "felt compassion" (Luke 10:33 NASB). The Samaritan traveled well because he *felt* what the man at the side of the road felt. The Samaritan traveled with compassion, and Jesus wanted his listeners to take notice.

In his wonderful book entitled *Compassion*, the late Cath-. olic writer Henri Nouwen reminds his readers that the word *compassion* is derived from the Latin words *pati* and *cum*, which together mean "to suffer with."[1] He writes, "Compassion asks us to go where it hurts, to enter into places of pain, to share in brokenness, fear, confusion, and anguish. Compassion challenges us to cry out with those in misery, to mourn with those who are lonely, to weep with those in tears."[2] Thus when Luke writes that the Samaritan's heart was moved, we meet a man of compassion. And Jesus illustrates a point with this man: *engage with those encountered along the way.*

Thomas Merton, another Catholic writer, uses slightly different language to expand on this notion of compassion. Merton believed that compassion is "a keen awareness of the interdependence of all these living beings, which are all part of one another."[3] If we embrace the notion that all of life is interdependent, then we must believe that everyone is our neighbor—regardless of race, social status, or geography—and that we are not islands living an isolated existence. The Samaritan, by allowing his heart to be moved, demonstrated this interdependence. He stopped for a stranger because he felt the stranger's pain as his own. And because he could empathize with the stranger's pain, he could not just walk on by.

Samuel and Pearl Oliner, a couple who did extensive research on rescuers of Jewish Holocaust victims, were curious to understand why certain non-Jewish citizens risked their lives, careers, and friends to save endangered Jewish people. When the Oliners compared the Empathy Scores (in a psychological test used to measure levels of empathetic responses to various life situations) of rescuers with those of nonrescuers, they found no particular differences between the two groups on such measures as shared feelings, affection, anxiety, pleasure, humor, or susceptibility to the moods of others. One difference, however, stood out. The rescuers had a strong tendency to be *moved by pain*. "Sadness and helplessness aroused their empathy,"[4] claimed the Oliners. At some point in their lives, the rescuers had developed the capacity to connect with and to be moved by another person's pain. This capacity to connect with another's pain was what compelled them to reach across racial and legal barriers to protect Jewish people. The ability to *feel* pain led to action.

CONTEMPLATING COMPASSION

Why does Jesus tell the story of the Samaritan? Why does Jesus want his listeners to embrace this image of an unlikely hero who responds in an unlikely manner? I believe Jesus wanted to provide us with this image because it captures the essence of faithful living. If you let the Samaritan's story take up residence in your heart, you will continually be reminded to travel life's road in a way that reflects the nature of God.

Christian theologian Meister Eckhart reminds us that "Whatever God does, the first outburst is always compassion."[5] Whether it is God hearing the cries of the Jewish people in Egyptian captivity or Jesus stopping to heal the blind and the broken, we see God's compassion affirmed throughout Scripture. Jesus himself says, "Be compassionate, just as your Father is compassionate" (Luke 6:36 NLT), underscoring our need to exercise compassion and the exciting truth that *God is compassionate.*

But compassion does not begin and end with feelings. As in the story of the good Samaritan, *feeling with* another should lead to *action.* It is the beginning of a response. Jesus did not conjure clever stories of a Samaritan to say, "Look at this great guy; his heart was moved by the needs of the man by the side of the road." What Jesus was saying was that the response—the taking care of another's needs—begins with identification. It is not enough to just feel bad about someone or some situation. One must respond.

We are all acutely aware of self-serving, selfish people in the world. The pool of humanity holds plenty of examples of those who have lost the capacity to *feel with* others. Probably even more could be found who feel but choose not to act. This is why we must work at noticing Samaritans in our daily lives. Doing so will puncture our bubbles of comfort and call us into action. And when we see gentle, heroic compassion exercised in ordinary places, we must invite those images to reside in our hearts, inspiring us to respond in ways that reduce pain and suffering in our world.

STORIES OF COMPASSION NOTICED

Compassionate people surround us. Often they are lost in the shadows of those who live in the spotlight. They are not the celebrity types who embrace the popular social justice cause. Nor are they the athletes who show up to the charity event to do an interview. Truly compassionate people are those who go about their business quietly and faithfully. These saints are helping in soup kitchens, hospitals, and classrooms. They are the people who stop for the person with the flat tire or ask the new church visitor home for lunch. Without any fanfare they cross social boundaries and share their resources with strangers. They lead with their hearts, not the socially prescribed rules that govern the actions of so many. We must find these folks in the shadows—not because they need our attention but because we need to see how they live compassionately. A few of these saints have crossed my path. Every time I meet one of these good Samaritans, I am challenged to remember Jesus's call.

The Compassionate Priest

Those who, in the biblical phrase, would save their lives—that is, those who want to get along, who don't want commitments, who don't want to get into problems, who want to stay outside of a situation that demands involvement of all of us—they will lose their lives. What a terrible thing to have lived quite comfortably, with no suffering, not getting involved in problems, quite tranquil, quite settled, with good connections politically, economically, socially—lacking nothing, having everything. To what good? They will lose their lives.

Oscar Romero

Father Michael Doyle, a priest who stands about five feet tall and speaks with a thick Irish brogue, is one of my heroes. He's a joyful man who always sees beauty in life—even though his parish is surrounded by tremendous brokenness and pain.

For the past thirty years Father Doyle has been the head priest at Sacred Heart Catholic Church on the south side of Camden, one of the poorest communities in America. Camden is crouched against the great Delaware River and is glutted by scrap yards, a sewage treatment plant, a trash-to-steam plant, and hundreds of abandoned homes and factories. On a hot August day one is reluctant to breathe because the air is so foul.

Father Doyle was *assigned* to South Camden (no one's notion of a promotion) because of his outspoken views on the Vietnam War. As an associate priest in a large, affluent, suburban parish, he was banished to the badlands since the church powers saw him as a troublemaker. But rather than becoming bitter, Father Doyle committed his life to working with the poor, trying to bring dignity and justice to their lives. He initiated housing programs and feeding ministries (he doesn't have people suffer the humiliation of standing in soup lines; rather, they are waited on at tables with tablecloths) and began political activism. He was and is a light in our community.

One always is hearing stories about Father Doyle. One of my favorites is about the time he paid the liquor store owners around his church to stay closed until noon on Sunday—so all the neighborhood alcoholics could go to Mass.

The other day I bumped into Ernie, an old friend of Father Doyle who has known him for years. "Father Mike's a saint, ya know," he began. "He's the reason I believe in God."

"A saint?"

"Well, yes. It was back in the seventies that Father Doyle, the Berrigan brothers (who were famous radical priest activists), and a few others were protesting the draft." My interest was piqued, for something about those protest years has always intrigued me.

Ernie continued. "They were planning ways to disrupt the draft because they were convinced it was unjust. Of course, they didn't believe in the war, and they were appalled by the disproportionate number of minorities being pulled from our cities to be drafted to fight." Ernie took a breath and looked up toward the sky as if remembering.

"The FBI, who had been monitoring the group, got to one of the protesters. They made a deal with him and sent him back into the group as an informant. For the next few months the man provided enough information for the FBI to bring a case against the group. The protesters eventually went to court and narrowly missed receiving serious prison sentences."

As I listened to Ernie tell the story, I found it difficult to understand how being a protester who narrowly missed conviction made anyone a saint. Courageous, perhaps. A man of conviction, certainly. But a saint?

"But here's the kicker," continued Ernie with intensity. "One day while the court proceedings were taking place, the informant's eight-year-old son fell out of a tree, landed on a fence, and was killed. Needless to say, the informer was devastated. But guess who was there every night after the court proceedings to minister to that devastated man and his family? You're right. Father Doyle. Now that's a saint in my book."

Ernie's story didn't surprise me; it only confirmed what I already knew. Not only was Father Doyle a radical who spoke up for what he believed, but he also embodied and lived out the Christian virtues of compassion and forgiveness. He saw his enemy in pain and reached out as an agent of healing.

Jesus told us to love our enemies and pray for those who persecute us (Matt. 5:44). But isn't it always easier to speak those words than to live them out? And for anyone who does live out those words, it is always exhilarating to know that what seems to be *impossible* for us is actually quite *possible* with God. Father Doyle demonstrated that compassion for another hurting human being is possible, even when that hurting human being is hurting you.

One of my all-time favorite stories and musical dramas is Victor Hugo's *Les Miserables*. Near the beginning of the story is a powerful encounter between Jean Valjean and a priest. Valjean has just escaped from prison and seeks asylum in the rectory of a church. Graciously, the priest takes him in. In the middle of the night, Jean Valjean decides to steal the expensive silverware from the rectory. He has the heart of a criminal and is apprehensive about his future with no money and no job prospects. He packs the antique silverware into a bag and heads off with his loot. But Valjean is captured by a police officer and brought back to the priest. The officer shows the priest what Valjean has stolen and asks the priest if he desires to throw him into jail.

In one of the most powerful moments in the story, the priest looks for a long moment at Valjean and says, "You forgot to take the candlesticks as well." Both Valjean and the officer are completely caught off guard. Consequently, Valjean is released by the police. This expression of grace becomes the defining moment in Valjean's redemption. He goes on to completely change his life and becomes a person who displays compassion to others. His remarkable transformation begins with the priest's willingness to forgive and display lavish, undeserved love.

Saints are not people who store up goodness, or people who live perfect lives. Rather, saints are people who are quick to forgive and display compassion. What a different place our world would be if there were more "saints."

Acting with compassion is difficult, even when you like a person. To act compassionately toward a person who betrays you gives this command a whole new dimension. I am not sure I could do what Father Doyle did. His testimony pierces my heart. But what Father Doyle teaches me is that it is possible to be truly compassionate.

The Compassionate Community

Come to me, all you who are weary and burdened, and I will give you rest.

Matthew 11:28

Friday morning chapel. The less-than-enthusiastic teenagers slouched into the room that doubled as the history classroom. It was 8:15—and everyone believed that even God wasn't awake till 9:00. Some placed their heads on their desks, not ready to deal with school yet. Others gossiped about weekend plans. Teachers shushed the students. A spiritual epiphany seemed unlikely this morning. Chapel was just a chore.

"Listen to this sentence from the Bible," began Mr. Bell tentatively. He doubted there would be any rustling of angels' wings this morning. He opened to an earmarked page, slid his finger down the page, and read in a deep, rich voice, "Come to me, all of you who are weary and carry heavy burdens, and I will give you rest." He closed the Bible and leaned on the edge of the desk at the front of the room. He paused and intently looked at the sleepy, disinterested gathering.

"Do you have any burdens? Are you tired of carrying them?" It was like ice water tossed on them. The boys in the back defensively snickered, hoping to rally the others. "We're going to talk about feelings in a classroom? Get real!" one could just imagine them whispering.

Mr. Bell said, "Settle down, guys."

An awkward silence came over the room. Mr. Bell waited.

"My younger sister moved out of the house last week," began fourteen-year-old Tia in practically a whisper. One of the back-row boys muttered, "Good for her," provoking chuckles. But Tia was not deterred. "She's living with my dad, and I'm worried about her safety. I don't get to see her." Tia began to cry. Nobody in the room breathed.

Another hand shot up. "I'm worried about my mom," voiced Sergio. "She has two jobs, and she still can't keep up. . . . She's under a lot of pressure. And then there's my younger cousin. He's got no father. He's headin' to make some big mistakes."

Victor interrupted. "My mom's always locked in her room. I can't get her to come out. She's really depressed. I hate to see her like that."

"Yeah, well, my father just got out of jail," said Rhonda. "Been there for years. I'm afraid of him. And you can bet it'll be drugs again. I wish I could help him, but I can't." She paused. "We really don't have anything in common. I don't like him. I just don't."

There was a long, airless pause.

There were tears. The laughter had stopped.

Then Poncho: "My brother doesn't take school seriously. He's lazy, doesn't study. I'm worried—worried he'll drop out and start selling drugs."

Almost helplessly, Toby said his younger sister doesn't even go to school anymore. "And she stole sixty dollars from me last week. She and Mom are always fighting. I just don't know what to do anymore. It makes me sad to think about it."

For the next thirty minutes the students poured out their hearts to one another and their teachers—sharing their burdens and telling of the things that really wearied them.

Those rough-edged teens hugged one another, cried with one another, and prayed for one another. In those sacred moments they were safe. They had become the church for each other.

Our teachers have continued to talk about "the chapel" that created a whole new direction for the kids and our school. "It's as though we became a community. The kids really began to care for one another and identify with one another's pain. They're no longer the same," Mr. Bell shared later at the staff meeting.

The apostle Paul wrote to the church of Galatia that they should "bear one another's burdens, and in this way you will fulfill the law of Christ" (Gal. 6:2 NRSV). *The law of Christ?* Why did Paul use such weighty language when describing the act of carrying one another's burdens? Why did he associate the act of burden carrying with the law of Christ? Perhaps it was because Paul realized that the health and vitality of the Christian community was somehow linked to this unique practice of looking beyond ourselves and sharing the pain of our brothers and sisters. Certainly Paul realized that when we share our pains and worries, our relationships move to a much deeper level. And as our relationships move to that deeper level, true community becomes possible.

The depth of pain our students carry in their young hearts staggers my imagination and humbles me. Their stress, their worries, their burdens are beyond comprehension. How do they function, let alone pay attention in class?

Yet somehow, in their sea of unfairness, those kids demonstrate something powerful for us all. They show us that we may not be able to eliminate our burdens and our worries, but we can "feel with" others and bear with them together as we respond to Jesus's invitation to come to him—and the burdens can become a little lighter, a little easier to manage. And in so responding to him and one another, we fulfill the law above all laws: Christ's law of love.

I recently read that more and more young people are turning to the Internet for their spiritual nourishment. Why? Because they can be truly honest. They can ask honest questions, share their deepest doubts, and reveal their hurts without being rejected or embarrassed! Christian fellowship should be a place where we can be vulnerable. That's because, as we learn from the teens at our high school, when we act vulnerably we can respond with compassion toward one another. How can you create places where hurting people can be vulnerable?

I Didn't Want to Take a Chance

Compassion is a kind of fire (Aquinas says compassion is the fire that Jesus came to set on the earth)—it disturbs, it surprises, it ignites, it burns, it sears, and it warms. Compassion incinerates denial; it especially warms and melts cold hearts, cold structures, frozen minds, and self-satisfied lifestyles. Those who are touched by compassion have their lives turned upside down. That is not necessarily a bad thing.

Matthew Fox

"I'll tell ye one of th' most memorable moments of my life," began Ian, a burly Scotsman with tattoos on his arms and a beautiful brogue for telling a story. Ian had begun his life in a poor family but had worked to become a successful businessman. Now he had a small hotel in northern Scotland and was hosting a group of American visitors.

The evening had been full of stories and laughter. "You'll like this one, Bruce," Ian winked at me from the other end of the table, "you being religious and all that."

I had been introduced as a clergyman and thus had been singled out to perform all the "religious" duties—such as prayers before meals—and had become the person everyone politely apologized to when they cursed or made an off-color comment. Since this was not exactly a Sunday school crowd,

I had heard a few "Sorry, Rev, I forgot you were here"–type comments throughout the evening.

Ian began, "One night I was driving down highway A-26 with my good friend Thor. We were moving along pretty well. We drove under a bridge and all of a sudden my friend yells, 'Stop! Stop!' I pulled the car over to the side of the road. There was a bedraggled woman there in obvious need." Ian paused for a dramatic moment while he took another sip of his ale.

"Thor said, 'Wait here.'

"Before I could say anything, Thor jumped out of the car and walked back along the road toward the woman. Out of my rearview mirror, I saw the woman sitting under the bridge holding a cardboard sign. On it was scribbled, 'I need food and medicine for my baby.' She really seemed destitute. She was dirty and had an old blanket wrapped around her. A few minutes later Thor jumped back into the car and abruptly said, 'Let's go.'"

The men sitting around the table all had their eyes fixed on Ian. He had captured the moment. "'What'd you do?' I asked Thor when he got back into the passenger seat.

"'I gave 'er fifty pounds,' my friend replied.

"'Are you crazy?' I responded in disbelief. 'She'll only use it for drink or drugs. Ya shouldn'ave done that.'"

At this point in the story Ian's eyes began to fill with tears. His voice became quiet. "D'ya know what my friend said?" said our storyteller in a whisper. "He said, 'I know . . . but I jes didn't want ta take a chance.' Those words have just stayed with me over the years," concluded Ian to the group. "Since then Thor has died, but that moment is fixed in my mind like a Polaroid snapshot. That man had a heart o' gold."

The twelve of us sitting around the table were silent, the earlier laughter and joking gone. We had been moved by the story. We had all walked away from needs and cries by the roadside rather than responding with compassion as Thor did.

I later pondered that the important part of Ian's story did not center on what the destitute woman did with the money. The important part of the story was the impact that Thor's act of giving had on *Ian*. The fifty pounds was irrelevant, whether the woman had used it wisely or wasted it. What was relevant was the fact that this spontaneous act of generosity deeply impacted Ian, and later his guests, and has continued to guide the way Ian uses his resources. Thor's simple gesture of compassion was more powerful and more memorable than a sermon or a Scripture—especially for a man like Ian who hardly ever darkens the door of a church. Ian's life was gently and significantly altered because of Thor's act of compassion. I wish that I could say that I am always a generous giver. I wish I could say that I embody Thor's willingness to give because he *did not want to take a chance*.

After twenty years in urban ministry, I find my heart getting a little crusty. Having been scammed and manipulated by seemingly needy people in every possible way, I find that consequently my compassion and giving have become guarded and calculated. The organization I direct used to run a food pantry. But I found that men took the food we gave them down the street and sold it for drug money. After a while I reluctantly shut down the pantry. Likewise, I've had mothers cry on my shoulder for money to be used for their asthmatic babies, only to see them later in the day coming out of a liquor store with bottles of cheap bourbon. I have begun to develop a cynical edge, and my spirit of giving and generosity has slowly eroded.

Of course I know that I am to use wisdom in my giving. Being a good steward of what God has given me is important. But what is more dangerous—allowing my heart to become cynical and closed or erring on the side of "taking a chance" and maintaining a spirit of compassion? Ultimately, I think we are to reflect a kind of love that moves beyond common sense—a love that gives people a glimpse of God's *unconditional love*. That's the kind of love Jesus talked about in Luke 6 when he called his disciples to "give to everyone who asks" (v. 30) and "do good to those who do good to you" as well as to those who *don't* do good to you (vv. 33, 35).

Jesus calls us to a higher form of love—a love that is compassionate to all and willing to take a chance on people others overlook.

I often struggle with people who beg for spare change by the side of the road. If I give, I wonder if I have truly helped or have just fed someone's addiction or dependency. Being a "good steward" of my resources is important, but I also know that I can hide behind this logic. Thor's response of "I didn't want to take a chance" is a prophetic word for all of us whose hearts might be a little cynical. Our "good stewardship" must never replace our compassion.

> Lord,
> Help us to notice expressions of compassion in our
>   world.
> Open our eyes to those saints who lead with their
>   hearts,
> bleeding goodness on those who are broken,
> frightened, and alone in this world.
> And when we see the spirit of compassion at work,
> move us to do likewise.
> Amen.

7

Courage Noticed

Daughter, your faith has healed you. Go in peace and be
freed from your suffering.

Mark 5:34

The topic for the dinner speakers was "Life's Big Mistakes
and What I've Learned." Most offered funny stories
followed by a short word of wisdom. A restauranteur told
about dropping a soufflé on the lap of a famous celebrity
patron. An auto manufacturer shared his mistake on an
automotive part, ultimately costing millions of dollars, with
the lesson, "If I'd only listened to my machinist." These were
good after-dinner laughs, but the lessons learned were less
than profound.

But then an unknown guest who sat near the head table
spoke up, giving her name as "Florence, but everyone calls
me Flo." She described herself as a stay-at-home mom who
in her midfifties discovered unique abilities as a photogra-

pher and writer. "It wasn't too late to re-create myself," she said proudly.

"The biggest mistake of my life, however, was earlier, when I did not have the *courage* to speak up for what I knew to be true."

Florence was no Ralph Lauren or Laura Ashley model, but she had southwestern good taste and soft graying hair. But it was her serious tone that stilled the guests' clattering dessert spoons. Her British accent helped create a certain tranquility in the room. "I had just delivered my second child," she continued, breaking the silence with a piercing seriousness. "We were visiting the States. My husband was on a teaching assignment in Boston. I was away from home and knew no one. The hospital was foreboding, sterile, and strange. I had the sense that something had gone wrong. I looked up from the delivery table to see the doctor walking out of the delivery room with my child wrapped in a white linen cloth."

Florence paused again, seeking control. No one breathed. "I weakly called to the doctor to come back. 'I want to hold my child . . . I need to touch him. He's a part of me. I need to say hello to my baby.'

"The doctor called back, 'Don't worry, don't worry. I'll take care of everything. Just rest! It's *not* a good idea for you to hold the child.' The doctor disappeared behind the doors. That was 1960. I was young. Physicians were gods, so I silenced my inner voice. I never saw the doctor or my child again. That moment haunted me for thirty years after my return to England."

Not only had there been no closure to the event, but Florence knew nothing of what had happened to her still-born baby. The hospital offered no details. "My biggest mistake back then was not standing up to the doctor," she confessed to the hushed room of strangers. "I knew what I should have done, what I *wanted* to do, and yet I didn't do it. I was afraid. I should have *demanded* to see my child! I was so young."

Much to the relief of the audience, Florence's story did not end there. At the age of fifty-five, she returned to the United States, returned to the hospital where her child had been born, and found the records including where he had been buried. After thirty years of deep regret, Florence visited the grave. She touched the earth at her child's grave, wept, and told her son good-bye.

"Now I've learned that I must have the courage, whatever the circumstances, to give voice to what I know to be true. I lived too many years in silence, not sharing my feelings and my opinions—not standing up to those who 'know' what is best for me."

Through their tears the audience stood, applauded, and cheered.

We had identified with Flo and her struggle to be courageous that night. How many times had we been in situations where we should have voiced our thoughts but held our tongues, deferred to "experts" out of fear or a lack of confidence? I left the auditorium feeling quite drained but with a new desire to be more courageous.

NOTICING COURAGE

Courage strengthens our will to act in ways that cut against the tide of the status quo and helps us to make difficult, sometimes costly, decisions. Meeting ordinary people who act courageously provides examples of how we might live more courageously ourselves. In the Gospel of Mark, chapter five, Mark writes about Jesus *noticing* an act of true courage and then affirming it by calling it an example of faith. At the center of the story was a woman who had been experiencing vaginal hemorrhaging for twelve years. Consequently, because of the taboos of her culture, she had lived as an invisible person in the shadows. Her bleeding, according to the customs of the time, had made her unfit for human contact.

Living as a rejected person profoundly impacts any person's self-worth, self-esteem, and sense of place. Living as a fringe person can create severe inferiority—a sense that one is worthless, with no rights. I can only imagine that the bleeding woman in Mark's story fits the profile. Because of her rejected position in society, her compelling act of courage was remarkable. She was determined: "I *will* touch the holy man. He *will* heal me." She had hope in Jesus and a stubborn refusal to be shackled by the confines of the religious legalisms of her day.

Ms. Ruby Sales, who directs a social justice ministry in Washington, DC, that gives voice to oppressed people, receives courage from the testimony of the woman in Mark's Gospel. Sales writes,

> The unnamed woman with the flow of blood has been "buked and scorned." Her infirmity is not just the flow of blood, as physically debilitating as that was. According to her tradition, a woman with menstrual flow is unclean and therefore must be isolated for seven days. This particular woman has been constantly bleeding for twelve years—meaning twelve years socially stigmatized and isolated, cut off from her community, her community cut off from her.[1]

Socially stigmatized for over a decade! That meant going to the market in the late afternoon when no one was there; drawing water during the hot part of the day, when no one else was around; standing outside the synagogue, never allowed inside, sure she had been cut off from God; and missing out on physical intimacy—no hugs and no touching. It meant living with shame, inferiority, and diminished worth every day.

My life certainly has been easy in comparison: raised in a loving family, enjoying the privileges of society's dominant racial and religious groups, never persecuted because of some social stigma. Yet despite those privileges, I can still struggle to feel fully confident when approaching people whom society deems as powerful and important. (Interrupting the day of a "holy man or woman" to seek their help—let's say a Nelson Mandela, an Archbishop Desmond Tutu, a Mahatma Gandhi, a Mother Teresa—is not something I, or many of us, would do.)

And yet, from her position of obscurity and rejection, the ailing woman reached out and touched Jesus, the man leading the procession! She pushed through the crowd and asserted herself. She mustered up the courage to overcome her fear and touched just the edge of Jesus's clothes. She purposely performed a subversive act, and it had serious implications. Touching Jesus, according to the prevailing customs, would *contaminate* him. By touching him, the woman was infecting Jesus—making a holy man ceremonially unclean. She did something she knew she was not supposed to do, and even though she tried to disappear into the anonymity of the crowd, she remained true to her inner hope—her belief that Jesus would heal her.

Jesus could have paid her no attention, but he came to an abrupt stop, turned around, and softly asked, "Who touched me?" The disciples, not paying very much attention at the moment and being impressed by the shouting crowd, thought the question was a joke. "Oh, come on, Jesus, there's a mob crowding around us." They were unaware of the woman's extraordinary act of courage and faith. "Jesus," wrote Mark, "kept looking around to see who had done it" (5:32). Mark portrays a Jesus who wanted to notice and wanted to freeze-frame history so his followers could be treated to a living image of faithfulness. Jesus sensed that he was in the presence of courage and wanted to acknowledge the gift of faith he had received.

Ruby Sales comments on this drama that the woman "refuses to be captive, to accept her unworthiness. She refuses to believe that she does not have a place and membership in the community. In going forth to find Jesus, she is doing more than seeking a restoration of health. She is calling into question the social ordering of relationships, including the use of religious law and sacred tradition to regulate those relationships. Ultimately, she is challenging the very nature of her community—who the community is with each other, and who the community is with God."[2]

Note the significant fact that Mark's drama is explicit about crediting the woman's healing to *her faith*, not to Jesus's power. "Daughter," claimed Jesus, "your faith has healed you" (v. 34). And I believe this is what Jesus wants us to notice: experiencing the presence of God is not something that just magically happens. To experience the presence of God, a person must move toward God in courage, faith, and hope. As we move toward God, we begin to experience God more fully. The woman knew that she must confront social and religious barriers, but she courageously crossed them and demonstrated to both Jesus and the crowd that God's presence is never restricted to the groups of people who have been "approved" by other humans or institutions. God's grace and presence are realities for all to experience.

CONTEMPLATING COURAGE

Frequently throughout the Gospel narratives, we see the phenomenon of courage and faith working hand in hand. They are like partners who work and move together.

I once heard a compelling definition of faith that illustrates this idea: *faith is putting ourselves in situations where if God does not show up, we are in trouble.* Moses led the people of Israel to the edge of the Red Sea and experienced the miracle of a parted sea. Shadrach, Meshach, and Abednego refused to bow down to King Nebuchadnezzar and were delivered from the fiery furnace. Biblical acts of faith are often also acts of courage. God shows up when people courageously step out to confront injustice and give witness to God's reign in the world.

How then do we become courageous people? Courage is initially cultivated when we *notice* people who *demonstrate* courage. Through noticing and contemplating acts of courage, we find ourselves examining our own lives and our own decisions. We thus begin to realize that courage is not always about standing up to evil empires, engaging in heroic battles with tyrannical dictators, or climbing Mount Everest. Rather, courage is demonstrated in the small choices of our daily lives.

Pulitzer Prize–winning poet Maya Angelou believes that courage is *the* great virtue. Angelou talks of courage this way:

> I think that we're in the presence of courage when we see a person during cruel times being kind. We know we're in the presence of courage when everyone is on the run, ideas are on the run, everything is fluid, everything is volatile, and a person has the patience, gives herself or himself time, to allow someone else to have time. That is courage. In a time of greed, when to have more means to be more, and someone is generous—instead of taking in, is giving out—that is courage. When war is being threatened or promised, when there's much waving of knives and brandishing of cannons and rattling of sabers, and a person talks about peace, that's courage.
>
> Without courage you can't practice any other virtue consistently—you can't be consistently fair, kind, generous, patient without courage.[3]

Angelou's definition of courage reveals the many faces of this virtue and speaks of the many ways to express courage at our jobs, in our communities, and in our relationships. Whether it is risking our job by taking a truthful stand on a company policy, embracing a neighbor whom others have rejected, standing up to a politician who is not representing the best interests of the community, or facing unpleasant truths about ourselves and our past—all take courage. But it is in our acts of courage that we begin to find our truest selves. It is in our acts of courage that we maintain our integrity and nourish our souls. And it is in our individual and collective acts of courage that we begin to find healing for ourselves and help others to heal. Through our acts of courage we provide channels for the presence of God to move in the world.

STORIES OF COURAGE NOTICED

Why do we need to find people of courage? Because courage is infectious and courageous people act as prophetic examples for how courage works in a complex world with complex decisions that continually challenge our integrity and moral judgment. Theorizing about right and wrong is easy. So is imagining what we should do in difficult situations. But acting out courageous decisions is something quite different. I believe the best way to understand courage is to watch it unfold in the actions of ordinary people. I need to meet people who embody this virtue in their daily lives. Sure, we read in our history textbooks about people who shaped the course of history with their courage. But these people can seem distant and far removed from our lives. I hope the people in the following stories will inspire you to live more courageously.

The Courage to Deliver

The great spiritual task facing me is to so fully trust that I belong to God that I can be free in the world—free to speak even when my words are not received; free to act even when my actions are criticized, ridiculed, or considered useless; free also to receive love from people and to be grateful for all the

128

signs of God's presence in the world. I am convinced that I will truly be able to love the world when I fully believe that I am loved far beyond its boundaries.

Henri Nouwen, *Beyond the Mirror*

"How'd your day go?" I said flatly as I came through the door and gave my wife a peck on the cheek. She had already started dinner.

"Well, I dropped by Kay's house today." I gave her a mindless nod, trying to give the impression that I was interested. After a day dealing with people's problems—and I was sure this was going to be another one—I wasn't really in the mood. But I did my best to pretend as I made my way to the refrigerator to get a cold soda.

Pam continued, "I decided to get Kay some flowers today. I needed to see how she was holding up." I smiled and opened the soda.

Just that morning we had learned that Kay's husband was in the late stages of a brain tumor. He had only weeks to live. And I was not surprised at Pam's response. Giving flowers is one of her gifts—she really enjoys putting together colorful bouquets for people who need a little cheering up.

"Kay wasn't home," she said, "so I left the flowers with her son-in-law, Henry. He told me that Kay has been going to the hospital every day. Gets there around ten and stays till nine." I sat at the kitchen table, put my feet up on a chair, and took a big gulp of my soda. My attention was still wandering as I thought about all the loose ends at work.

"I asked him," Pam continued, "if I should visit her at the hospital. He advised against it—said she really didn't want to see anyone. So I left the flowers with him, and asked him to be sure to tell her that our thoughts and prayers are with them."

If I had been Pam, that would have been the end of the story; my mission would have been accomplished. The flowers and the note I left would have communicated my concern and love. But, as I've learned over the years, my wife and I are different. Her story was just beginning. "I got in the car and began to drive home," she said. She paused for a moment, as if she were unable to put into words what she was thinking. "Then something flashed into my mind . . . maybe not a flash . . . more like a compulsion. I felt—no, I *knew* God was telling me that I was supposed to go to the hospital and give Kay a special message personally."

My theology departs from my wife's at this point. It's not as though I don't believe in prophetic messages or audible heavenly voices, but I'm pretty cynical about their abuses. "Um, what was the message you were supposed to share?" I reluctantly asked and braced myself.

"Well . . . I just knew—it was a compulsion, really—that I was supposed to tell Kay, 'God hears you.'"

"*God hears you!* That was it?" I said, somewhat amused, maybe exasperated—for I had guessed that her story was going to be a little more dramatic, not just three simple words! Anyway, it hardly seemed to me like a message from God! No thunder. Nothing falling off a shelf, no doors rattling. Nothing. "You were going to drive all the way into the city to tell Kay that God hears you?"

"Well, honey," she was being patient with me, "yeah, I drove all the way to the city." She gave me one of her exasperated looks, which I have grown accustomed to. "I know it sounds a little crazy, but that was it," she said. "I tried to suppress the message, but it just wouldn't go away. I felt compelled—so I turned around and went to the hospital."

At this point I wasn't sure what to think. But one thing's for sure, I would never drive an hour out of my way, fight downtown traffic, and spend forever trying to find a parking place just to share three words with someone—especially someone I did not know that well. Maybe a family member or a close buddy, but someone I didn't know very well? I would have rationalized the idea away. I would have convinced myself that the whole notion was absurd. But then again, I am not Pam.

The story continued. Pam told me how she picked up some sandwiches, some fresh fruit, and a few bottles of juice to take to Kay, whom she found sitting in the waiting area outside her husband's room.

"Needless to say, Kay was somewhat surprised to see me, but she seemed pleased. Then after our initial chitchat while nibbling on some grapes, she looked at me and asked, 'Why did you come, Pam?'"

Now I was intrigued. I couldn't imagine what Kay must have been thinking.

"I told her, 'I have a message for you, Kay,'" Pam continued. "'And what I'm about to tell you may sound a little strange—maybe absurd! "God hears you."' Kay just looked at me. Then she said, 'That's it?' I nodded. Then it happened. She broke down and began to cry. The tears flowed. Up till that point she had appeared really strong and in control, but now she just cried. I had no idea what was happening," Pam concluded.

My eyes were beginning to water as well as I thought about this woman dealing with the intense pain of losing her husband and now hearing Pam's curious message. "After the tears slowed down, Kay began to share with me," continued Pam. "She said, 'Did you know my first husband, Ron, died of cancer? I prayed then that I would never again have to go through the agony I experienced from his painful death. Years later, when I married Jack, I specifically asked God to allow me to die first if illness ever struck again. Now it appears that that is not going to happen—even though when Jack was diagnosed with cancer, I prayed that he might be healed. But then he developed a brain cancer that cannot be treated. Pamela, I've just gotten to a place where I don't believe that God hears me anymore. I've given up on prayer. But now—your message.'"

Needless to say, Pamela was surprised that her message was connecting so deeply. If only she had more words to share, a further explanation, but she had only "God hears you"—the only words that needed to be shared.

As I later thought about my wife's experience, I wondered how often I had missed opportunities to share with others God's messages of grace. In the midst of all Kay's suffering and pain, God had not forgotten her. God was listening. Even though Kay felt as if her prayers were not being answered and, worse, as if God had turned away, God had a message to give—a simple message, the message that she needed desperately. God just needed a messenger.

How often do our inhibitions get in the way of God speaking through us to others? How often does our unwillingness to seem like a fool stop us from sharing what needs to be shared? How often does our need to sound profound get in the way of just sharing a few simple words?

Too often we sit on our holy impulses and divine hunches. You know the kind—they're simple inklings about people at strange times, and we never respond, we never get in touch. Or we feel an urge to write a letter, but we watch television instead. Or we want to visit or call someone, but we neglect to make the effort. Can they be promptings of the Spirit? Yes. And, sadly, we miss the Spirit's prompting when we do not follow through.

It is true that God loves every person uniquely. The only problem is that human beings are often the vehicles God has chosen to deliver extraordinary messages of love and grace. How often do God's deliveries fall short of their destinations because of us?

"God hears you," God said to a woman who had all but given up. Fortunately, he found a responsive messenger to deliver the message.

I wonder how many times I have failed to "deliver" a word because I did not possess the courage to do so. I thought it might be embarrassing, or irrelevant, or cause ripples in a relationship. Pam challenges me to act on those promptings, even though they may make me look foolish and irrational. She reminds me of the potential blessings I may hold back if I refuse to act.

Swimming against the Current

Christians should be troublemakers, creators of uncertainty, agents of a dimension incompatible with society.

Jacques Ellul

The Bible is straightforward and honest about its heroes. Seldom are they portrayed as the confident, self-assured leaders we'd expect them to be. Rather, they're written about as men and women who are called by God to do some courageous act and who are crippled with fear and full of excuses. Moses, for instance, complained so much about his failures and shortcomings that God sent him an assistant for his mission (Exod. 3:11; 4:10, 13). Jeremiah, on the other hand, said he was too young to take on a significant task (Jer. 1:6). Gideon needed signs and assurances that God would really walk by his side (Judg. 6:17).

Obviously, many of God's great leaders struggled with *courage*. Too frequently they were filled with doubt, fear, and uncertainty. Joshua was asked to take over after Moses and lead the children of Israel into the Promised Land—a daunting task that involved all kinds of bold stands and extreme acts of courage. (Perhaps that is why there are three verses referencing courage in the first chapter of the book of Joshua. Joshua had to be reminded to "be strong and courageous" in verses 6 and 7. Then verse 9 reads: "Be strong and courageous. Do not be terrified; do not be discouraged, for the LORD your God will be with you wherever you go.")

Take the story of seventeen-year-old Amanda. She sat across from me at the dinner table one evening at her home. I was a guest of her parents. I asked a few perfunctory ques-

133

tions in order to get to know this impressive teenager: "How's your summer job working out?" and "How did your school year end up?" It was the school question that provoked her to share the extraordinary story of her last few months as a high school senior. I learned that her final days at her prestigious college prep school had been extraordinarily stressful and filled with conflict.

"One of my classmates stood up in the auditorium," she said, reliving the event, "and mockingly raised a question for our graduating class. Of course she knew the answer before she asked. With sarcasm in her voice, she turned to the students and asked, 'How many of you want a *dry graduation*?' She was really asking about who wanted alcoholic drinks at their graduation parties. Can you believe that I was the only one to stand up?" she said with some pain. "Everybody thought I was out of touch. No booze at a high school graduation? Get real."

Amanda told me that tradition at her school included parent-sponsored open-bar after-graduation parties in recognition of the students' rite of passage. The parents justified serving the alcohol at the parties by claiming that their kids were going to drink anyway—so why not serve it?

Amanda was uncertain about what to do about her classmate's confrontation. But after a summer of discovering deeper dimensions of her faith, Amanda had decided to make some radical changes. Her personal faith had started to make a difference in the way she lived. That's why she knew a wet graduation, even served by parents, was wrong and also incompatible with the principles of the school. She wanted her graduation to be a special time—not one where she spent the night tripping over inebriated friends.

"So," she said with a sigh, "I began to go around to each student personally. I asked them to sign a petition that said 'No alcohol at graduation parties.' At first many of them were reluctant to sign, but after I talked with them, they began to express what they *really* felt. Forty percent signed the petition that indicated that they wanted a dry graduation.

"Well, I was bold, I guess, because I requested some time at the next meeting of the school's trustees. I took my petition along with me, plus a copy of the school's mission statement. They had all either forgotten the statement or more likely never bothered to translate the Latin phrases about the school's calling to 'high levels of morality and character.'"

It is not every day that one sits in the presence of a high school student who cuts against popular opinion and attempts to overturn an enduring tradition—all by herself. Amanda's mood became somber. "I challenged the trustees to remember the importance of their role as leaders. 'Our school boasts about its academic achievements and national reputation,' I reminded them. 'Now I feel strongly that if you held the young women of this school to a comparable level of *morality* and *character*, then we would have something really to boast about! Can you sit silently by and endorse underage, illegal drinking?'"

The trustees had been caught off guard, she said quietly. They knew Amanda was right. They knew what they needed to do. The question was, would these leaders, despite the popular trends, act as courageously as Amanda had? Then something unexpected and surprising happened.

"At the end of the table was a trustee named Mr. Torrence," she continued. "He motioned to the chairman of the trustees that he would like to speak. 'Thank you, Amanda,' said Mr. Torrence, somewhat emotional. 'Thank you for your compelling words and work on behalf of the school. I only wish there had been a student as bold as you when I was in high school.' His eyes began to fill up with tears. The other trustees stared. Never had they seen their fellow trustee in such a state. After he choked back his tears, he continued. 'For the past thirty years I've struggled with an addiction. I am an alcoholic. I want you to know that it is of great significance that I took my first drink at my high school graduation.' He paused. 'I wish I never had.' Mr. Torrence's confession took everyone by surprise. The room went silent.

"By this time I knew I had one vote from the board. I thought that my presentation, coupled with the little talk of Mr. Torrence, would be enough to get all of the trustees on my side. But the trustees were tougher than I thought. They nixed my idea.

"The months leading up to my graduation were no fun," she continued after taking a deep breath. "I was the focus of all the hallway gossip and ridicule. One student even threw a chair at me. That was strange and scary. What hurt most was that I was dissed—you know, ignored—by my closest friends, and someone even graffitied my graduation picture displayed in the school lobby." Obviously Amanda had paid a considerable price for her stand. Sadly, she ended up not attending her graduation—an event she had worked toward and looked forward to for twelve years.

Some might sneer at the heroic actions taken by Amanda. After all, there are thousands of high school students who do not attend their graduations, and teen drinking is too much the norm. But Amanda's story challenges us—it took God-given strength for her to take a stand against the status quo and speak out about what she believed to be true. Amanda demonstrated courage, among other virtues.

It's easy to get caught in the trap of not seeing the heroes in the midst of one's daily life. We can look to the great visionary leaders and admire their courage from a distance. Abraham Lincoln, Rosa Parks, Martin Luther King Jr., and Winston Churchill all reach across time and inspire us. But sometimes their distance and their bigger-than-life acts of courage immobilize us. Consequently, we can justify our own inactivity and unwillingness to speak out—we deem our present circumstances as being less important than those of the Civil War, the civil rights era, or World War II.

Certainly our heroes provide examples of courage, but it is courage from a safe distance. In our starstruck admiration, we can become blind to the important moments of courage needed in our own daily lives and in our own communities.

I do not believe we are necessarily born courageous. Courage grows each time we step out and do what is right, what is just, and what is true. Courage means speaking out when we know that something is being done that is wrong. It means acting in ways that make our communities and workplaces reflect God's intentions for all people. It means creating families and schools that provide nurturing and loving space in which children can grow and get a great education. It means caring for the world God has lent us during our brief earthly pilgrimage. Courageous acts are not limited to heroes in movie dramas. Rather, courage can be demonstrated every day by schoolchildren and stay-at-home parents, CEOs and plumbers, pastors and struggling adolescents.

Amanda was a courageous person. Her courage cost her, just as Moses's and Joshua's courage cost them. It cost her dearly. But she told me with enthusiasm, "I wouldn't change a thing!"

Postscript: Amanda may not have changed the drinking rules for her graduating class, but after that graduation that she chose not to attend, three students were admitted to the hospital for alcohol poisoning. The police entered the house where the party was being held and confiscated the alcohol. The school is considering changing their postgraduation policy next year.

I think of the recent scandals in corporate America— Enron, Tyco, and WorldCom. Obviously, there were good people in these companies who were well aware of policies, practices, and events that violated the ethical standards of their company. Nothing was said. Not enough people raised their voices. Perhaps they were afraid—afraid of losing their jobs or afraid of persecution. For whatever reason, good people failed to act with courage. I admire a young woman like Amanda because she is establishing the practice of courage at an early age. Are there things you need to speak against in your school? Your place of work? Your church?

True to Myself

> It is for this reason that love for God begins not with
>   the desire for God,
> and not with seeking God,
> but by withholding ourselves from all other things.
> It begins with our refusal to give our love to any-
>   thing in this world,
> our decision to hold back, to renounce,
> because we realize that there is nothing in this world
>   that can fully satisfy us.

> Diogenes Allen

"Since I've done so well in real estate, I get people calling me all the time asking if I will invest their money," began my friend, "but I have no interest anymore. The desire is gone."

At one time Wayman would have jumped at the opportunity to find a new venture—a new opportunity to make a deal. As a young, successful real estate developer, Wayman has had a knack for buying bankrupt properties and turning huge profits. His thoroughness, timing, and gut instinct have given him a stellar record. He has made a great deal of money. He has made other people wealthy as well. He has been on the fast track—lots of traveling, power lunches, and time away from his family.

Then Wayman began to evaluate his life, asking some soul-searching questions. Was life just about accumulating more stuff—bigger houses, faster boats, sportier cars? Was life about bigger stock portfolios and a larger net worth? Something began to change. God got ahold of him.

"When I get involved in 'the deal,' something takes over," he confessed. "I don't express the side of myself that I think God wants me to express—the side of me that celebrates what God is doing in me."

I admired his introspection since many people never take the time to really think about their lives. Instead, they avoid the tough questions—those questions that conjure up fear, that challenge our identity, and that expose those darker areas of our lives—the areas that too often control us.

Wayman continued, "One day I had to ask myself, *What really brings me joy? What really energizes me? What makes me feel that God is alive and working?* I realized that it is not stuff. It is not the things that cost $10,000 or even $100,000. What I discovered were the things that really brought me joy: waking up early to see the sunrise, taking a walk through the neighborhood with my wife, inviting people over for a good meal. Those are the things that brought me joy."

It is one thing to live a pipe dream that someday we will acquire wealth and prestige. It is different to have it and have the opportunity to have more and yet intentionally walk away from it. But Wayman jumped out of the frantic race for money and intentionally scaled back his lifestyle. He did this because his soul and his integrity were at stake. His goal was to live a more authentic life—a life built on a foundation of eternal values, not stuff with a temporary shelf life.

And Wayman is not alone to discover that it is hardly worth gaining the whole world only to discover that you forfeit your soul in the process (see Mark 8:36).

Just the other day I was listening to a National Public Radio interview with Sidney Poitier, the famous African American actor who played in groundbreaking Hollywood films such as *Guess Who's Coming to Dinner*, *The Defiant*

Ones, and *Lilies of the Field*—films that challenged negative portrayals of blacks in America and the racism that was still overt and rampant throughout our country. Poitier broke barriers by playing forceful and affecting characters who said something positive, useful, and lasting about our human condition. He is now in his midseventies.

Poitier had a less-than-auspicious start. Born in Nassau, Bahamas, he came to the United States when he was fifteen and landed in New York City with no money. He worked as a dishwasher. When he heard about an audition with the Negro Theatrical Company, he tried out for a part. His first audition was a flop. The people who saw him encouraged him to go back to washing dishes and give up on his dream of becoming an actor.

But Poitier persisted. He bought a radio so he could learn to speak "American" and lose his Bahamian accent. When he went back for a second audition, he met the same response. Those who watched the audition reinforced their earlier critique: "You do not have a chance at becoming an actor." But Poitier was a survivor. Although he seemingly could not act, he was perceptive. He noticed that the facility had no janitor. So he offered the administrators his services in exchange for the opportunity to watch other actors and study acting. He began to catch on.

What made Poitier's career so incredible were the roles he was able to land. During the late 1950s and 1960s, virtually the only acting jobs for African Americans in Hollywood were roles that affirmed existing stereotypes and promoted negative perceptions of people of color. Somehow, in the midst of that hostile and racist environment, Poitier was able to hold out for roles that did not demean him or the legacy of his parents.

When asked by the reporter why he did not accept the readily available demeaning roles, he responded, "I decided to live a life that reflected *my* values."

Poitier believed that what one does for a living articulates who one is. Consequently, his uncompromising beliefs excluded him from many roles and limited his exposure and opportunities for financial gain. But this did not matter to Poitier. He had a vision for his life.

Toward the end of the interview, the young NPR reporter asked Poitier why he was not doing more films. In a rather stern and direct voice, he replied, "Look, young woman. I'm seventy-three years old. I've been making movies for over fifty years. The only currency I have left is *time*. Why do I want to go over things that I've already gone over?"

While listening to Poitier's final words, I was overcome with the sense that I was listening to a man at peace with himself. Poitier knew who he was. He did not need more accolades, more recognition, or more awards. He was living a life that was true to himself. He had not departed from his vision.

Each of us can live lives that reflect our values. And there is something beautiful about a life that is aligned with eternal values. There is a centeredness that results in peace and contentment.

Our culture suggests that having *things* fills our inner emptiness. It is refreshing to find those who have the courage to say *enough is enough*. It is encouraging to meet those who have said no to the temptations of wealth and the accolades of the spotlight, being content to focus on things that really matter.

Living courageously is not just about speaking out on some issue or marching in a demonstration. Living courageously also means living a lifestyle that contradicts the illusion of our consumer culture. Wayman is a wonderful example of someone who demonstrates the relationship between courage and living with a greater sense of integrity. Poitier also teaches us about the importance of making decisions that do not violate our sense of integrity, even when doing so has a cost.

Lord,
Help me not to be governed by fear;
help me not to be bound by the expectations of
    others;
help me not to live in the cage of untruth;
I pray for courage:
courage to speak out;
courage to speak up;
and courage to act in ways that embody truth, faith,
    and love.
Amen.

8

CONTRITION NOTICED

Look, Lord! Here and now I give half of my possessions to the poor, and if I have cheated anybody out of anything, I will pay back four times the amount.

Luke 19:8

Do you remember me?"
Startled, I looked up from my desk. Standing there with his hands in his pockets was a young man of about thirty, I guessed. Was I experiencing memory loss? I nodded my head, extended a hand, and said, "Hey, buddy, great to see you!" He sensed my ambivalence.

"I worked here about ten years ago, was one of those interns." Hundreds of college-age interns had come through our doors over the years, so it wasn't easy to remember names.

"Umm, how long did you work with us?"

"About six months." I was still struggling because most of our interns stay a year. Then it hit me. This was the young

143

man who had abruptly left in anger and spewed all kinds of negative things about me and the way I managed. He also had subversively spread lies among our supporting churches and had complained to some of our donors. Oh, yes, yes, now I remembered Eddie, that *charming* young man who had left a trail of broken staff relationships and disenchanted contributors. It took me months to repair his wreckage.

"I just wanted to come by and say . . . *I'm sorry!*"

Surprised and amazed, I motioned for him to sit down in the chair next to my desk. His act of contrition had actually piqued my curiosity. Why on earth would he come back—after ten years—and apologize?

He cleared his throat; I knew he was uncomfortable. He said, "Back when I was here, I said a lot of mean things about you and the other staff. You may not believe this, but it's been weighing on my mind all these years. God's been working on me, and I just wanted to come by and clear things up. I'm really sorry about the trouble I caused."

Needless to say, I was stunned. Not every day does someone wander in off the streets and without any introduction barge into my office and apologize for things he or she said ten years earlier. Obviously his conscience had not been able to erase the past, and the wrong he had committed lingered like a bad dream, restricting his ability to grow in faith. Eddie wanted freedom. Eddie wanted to stand clean before the God who gives abundant life, who infuses us with vitality, who frees us so we can become the people we were created to be.

I assured him of my forgiveness and then asked, "So, what's been happening these past years?" Sadly, his past ten years had been riddled with many personal disappointments and failures—broken relationships, dead-end jobs, and a stifled spiritual life. It seemed that God had brought Eddie to a place where he needed to repair the past so that he could begin to construct a healthier future. I was part of his past destructiveness that needed repairing. Then we came to that awkward moment of silence when there was nothing left to share. Eddie stood, I reassured him of my forgiveness, we shook hands, he thanked me for listening, and then he walked out the door.

As I sat in the wake of this rather extraordinary confession, I found myself admiring this young man's efforts at reconciliation. To act upon the prompting of God's Spirit by coming back and apologizing took courage. I began to reflect. How many times had God's Spirit prompted me to do something and instead of responding, I simply suppressed the idea? Eddie embodied the practice of *contrition*—the act of showing remorse with a desire to amend the wrong committed. I not only had the opportunity to receive a brother's apology but also had the privilege of hearing a little of his motivation. More powerful than any sermon I had heard in recent months, Eddie's act of confession provided a serendipitous sermon in the middle of my workday. He had drawn me into his journey with God, and his actions could not easily be dismissed. I was challenged to think of the people I had wronged and the difficult situations I had swept under the rug. I had witnessed contrition—could I act in the same way?

ZACCHAEUS NOTICED

Luke's recording of Jesus's encounter with Zacchaeus (see Luke 19) is an invaluable illustration for God's children who desire to understand the nature of a contrite heart and the full ramifications of this concept called repentance. From this encounter we learn that Zacchaeus was an ordinary man who performed an extraordinary act of heart and will—an act that caught Jesus's attention and garnered a life-giving word of affirmation from Jesus. Zacchaeus remains worthy of our notice today.

Zacchaeus was a tax collector, wealthy because of his exorbitant, often illegal tax collecting. He was resented because of his close ties with the Roman government occupying Israel and his (and the government's) willingness to live off the backbreaking work of ordinary people. Certainly Zacchaeus was not sought after as a dinner guest by the religious leaders. So Jesus's inviting himself to Zacchaeus's house certainly raised eyebrows and excited the voracious rumor mill.

Not only was Zacchaeus resented, but Luke makes a point of referring to his stature—he was short. Why does Luke make the point? Some scholars argue that it simply explains the reason why short Zacchaeus, eager to see Jesus, climbed a tree. Other scholars argue that Luke and his audience lived in a world in which it was commonplace to associate outer physical characteristics with the inner qualities of people. In ancient literature, physical descriptions were often used to explain a person's actions and were designed to elicit certain feelings from the listening audience. A person like Zacchaeus would have been viewed as a laughable, perhaps despicable character because of his abnormal height. By using this description, Luke presents Zacchaeus as one of those contemptible characters. His occupation, his greed, and his physical stature combined to convince Luke's audience that this man was a "sinner indeed."[1] Most upright, *proper* people would ignore and avoid a man like Zacchaeus.

So Luke's verse 5 is significant: "When Jesus reached the spot, he *looked up* and said to him, 'Zacchaeus, come down immediately. I must stay at your house today'" (19:5, emphasis added). Jesus didn't walk past Zacchaeus in the tree, as it would have been easy to do since there was enough activity to keep Jesus's attention on the ground. People surrounded Jesus, bumped him, shouted questions, begged for healing or a word of wisdom, yet Jesus noticed Zacchaeus. Jesus *looked up* and saw a man who had made an extra effort to meet him.

Jesus understood what many of us usually miss: a man in a tree is never *just* a man in a tree. Or, to put it in contemporary terms, the student who acts out in sixth grade is never *just* a bad kid; nor is the college student who pierces every part of his body *just* into jewelry or the underachieving staff worker *just* lazy. There is usually a story behind the story. For Jesus, a wealthy, despised man climbing a tree to see him was a story worth noting and uncovering. Jesus *noticed*. Jesus stopped. Jesus looked up.

This interaction underscores Jesus's awareness of those people he passed in his travels—people often invisible to the crowds and disciples until Jesus singled them out and invited them into his space. Jesus displayed a willingness to uncover the true person hiding behind the labels (dastardly tax collectors!), the stigmas, and the stereotypes. He had an intuitive heart and a perceptive eye. While others walked with tunnel vision along the road, Jesus was noticing extraordinary happenings in the midst of the ordinary. With Zacchaeus, Jesus noticed a man who needed to be noticed.

By the end of Luke's telling of the story, we discover why Jesus stopped. Zacchaeus was not climbing trees just to get a glimpse of this holy man. Something deeper was driving him. Guilt, perhaps? An emptiness that couldn't be filled by money or notoriety? Would we call it an inferiority complex, self-loathing, perhaps? Whatever the case, Jesus embodied hope for Zacchaeus—the hope of being freed from the bondage of a guilty past and the hope and miracle of righting wrongs. Yet in order for the process of change to begin its course, Zacchaeus had to make a significant break from the old. In the presence of this traveling holy man who embraced him, Zacchaeus revealed a broken and contrite heart.

"Look, Lord! Here and now I give half of my possessions to the poor," cried Zacchaeus in an unusual expression of vulnerability, "and if I have cheated anybody out of anything, I will pay back four times the amount" (Luke 19:8). Upon hearing this remarkable confession, Jesus made a statement that must have raised the hair, turned the heads, and ignited the self-righteous tempers of those who heard. "Today," promised Jesus, "salvation has come to this house" (v. 9).

For those of us who read the Scriptures from a twenty-first-century perspective, it is important to realize that when Jesus spoke of "salvation," his hearers would understand the term within the framework of the Old Testament. The people of Israel did not make a distinction between the material and the spiritual world as we often do. Therefore, *salvation* was not simply a spiritual enterprise preparing people's souls for entry into heaven. Salvation, as understood by those listening at Zacchaeus's house, was anything that delivered people from circumstances or negative powers that prevented a full, joyous participation in community life.[2] In Zacchaeus's case, the "negative powers" he needed to be delivered from were the years of making a dishonest living, cheating his fellow citizens, and hiding cowardly behind the cloak of the Roman government. Zacchaeus had lived in the vise grip of a guilty conscience and years of wrongdoing. If he was going to enjoy the joy of community and love-based relationships, he needed to be open and honest.

Zacchaeus's confession revealed a person serious about changing himself. This was not mere lip service. Zacchaeus's net worth was about to be severely diminished. With each public reimbursement to his past victims, his past wrongs would be paraded throughout the community for all to see. Zacchaeus was committing financial and career suicide, yet he was willing to pay the price because his soul was at stake. And because he was willing to engage in this costly form of repentance, Jesus promised him freedom from the powers that were destroying his life. It is Jesus's promise—the promise of salvation to Zacchaeus's household—that identifies Zacchaeus as someone who needs to be noticed by all those who care about their relationship with God, their neighbor, and their community. Once again Jesus held up an ordinary man who performed an extraordinary act of practical faith and said to his listeners, "Take note!"

CONTEMPLATING CONTRITION

A pastor friend once told me, "Shallow repentance leads to shallow healing." By this he meant that if repentance is merely lip service, with no actions connected to the confession, then the confessor will experience little or no change in his or her life. Deep healing comes with deep confession and a willingness to make amends for the wrongs. Zacchaeus's contrition, by any measure, was costly.

In the twenty-first century we see high-profile people seeking forgiveness for past wrongs. CEOs of Fortune 500 companies seek forgiveness for embezzling millions of dollars. Politicians seek forgiveness for their misuses of power and position. Religious leaders seek forgiveness from those they have abused. Athletes seek forgiveness for gambling and sexual escapades. Entertainers seek forgiveness for indiscreet public actions. In our public cynicism, the question becomes, are these people really contrite? Should we embrace them back into the public community by offering trust and loyalty? How do we know when someone is really telling the truth? *Really* contrite?

Only God truly knows our hearts, so we must be careful when judging the authenticity of a person's contrition. But Zacchaeus's confession elicited a remarkably affirmative response from Jesus. Jesus believed Zacchaeus was on the right track. It wasn't that Zacchaeus was a better man than others. Public image and morality were not the issue. The issue was *salvation*—the release from powers that inhibit us from becoming the person God intends us to become. Zacchaeus was released from the debilitating, life-draining bondage of wrongdoing. Thus Zacchaeus had started the process of conversion in his life.

Diogenes Allen, in his important book called *Spiritual Theology*, helps flesh out the link between contrition and conversion. Allen notes that conversion is "not the terminus but merely the first stage of the Christian life."[3] He goes on to add that if we are to truly obey Jesus's commandment to love our neighbor as ourselves over a lifetime, "we have a great deal to do in the interval between our conversion and our death."[4] Allen's comments may be hard for some Christians to swallow. If we view our spiritual life only in terms of being "saved" or "unsaved," then we might be inclined to view repentance and conversion as *the* definitive moment in our spiritual life, not part of a longer salvation process—a process that, through a lifetime of contrite acts, releases the believer from those forces restricting us from full communion with God. Allen would agree that conversion is an important moment in our lives, but he would further challenge us to realize that conversion is only one stage in moving us closer to God. Therefore, Zacchaeus, in his act of contrition, began the process of true conversion by turning himself in a Godward direction. Jesus affirms this critical movement with the promise that "salvation" has come to his house.

All of us who desire this broader experience of salvation need to realize that acts of contrition in our daily lives will be part of the process. We need to realize that acts of contrition break the destructive tendencies of our personalities and transform those tendencies into roots that link us more intimately to the true source of life, God.[5] Unfortunately, our love affair with pride, self-centeredness, arrogance, meanness, blindness, and dishonesty can often grip us so tightly and embrace us so seductively that truly breaking their embrace on our lives through acts of contrition is difficult. Living examples from common people are needed to awaken us and spur us toward these courageous and often potentially humbling actions. The fact that Jesus noticed Zacchaeus's act of contrition is a reminder from history of the kind of costly confession needed to truly release ourselves from those forces that pull us farther away from God, farther away from our neighbors, and farther away from who God wants us to become. But what about examples from today? Do they exist? I believe they do. We just need to look. We need to *notice*.

STORIES OF CONTRITION NOTICED

We live in a world where we often hear public confessions. Athletes, movie stars, politicians, and religious leaders parade in front of TV cameras, seeking the public's forgiveness for things they have done wrong. At times it is very difficult to understand their motivation and their sincerity. Is their confession calculated to win votes? Sell books? Increase their box-office draw? It's hard to tell. We do know, however, that our inability to repent and show contrition is often our biggest hindrance to growing in faith. Our inability to say we're sorry and engage in appropriate acts of retribution is often connected to our pride and self-absorption. How do we become contrite people so that God's Spirit can fully dwell in our lives? I believe we can learn a great deal from watching those who implement this practice in their daily lives.

Dad, I've Never Forgotten

Inability to love is the central problem, because that inability masks a certain terror, and that terror is the terror of being touched. And if you can't be touched, you can't be changed. And if you can't be changed, you can't be alive.

James Baldwin

Roger Barnes was normally patient with his children. Seldom did he raise his voice. Never did he yell. He prided himself on controlling his temper and tried always to model self-control and love.

But this morning was a little different. Perhaps it was the coffee, or the way he slept—maybe some unconscious tension lingered from the previous day at work. Whatever the case, his kids were getting on his nerves.

At that moment Timmy knocked his bowl of Sugar Pops onto the floor; his sister Lisa went into hysterics. Roger lost it. Not only did he raise his voice—he yelled! Timmy and

151

Lisa sat stunned. Never had they seen their father so out of control. Their mother hurried the two children from the table and onto the school bus. They left their father, now calm, waving from the edge of the driveway.

Later that morning, just as Timmy's second-grade class was wrapping up its phonics lesson, the voice of the principal came over the public address system: "Timmy Barnes, please report to the office. Timmy Barnes, report to the office!"

Every eye turned toward Timmy Barnes as he reluctantly pulled himself up from his desk.

He began to think of everything he had done wrong in the past few days. *They didn't see me throw my apple core and miss the trash can, did they?*

As he slowly shuffled his way down the hall, he replayed every possible scenario. *It must have been the note I passed to Stevey Collins. That's got to be it.* Still at the age when a principal seems omniscient, Timmy believed that the ever-present, all-knowing Mr. Michaels had seen some misdeed. *Or someone had ratted!*

"You may sit over there," smiled the office secretary, Miss Schmidt—much too sweetly. She motioned him to sit on the wooden bench. The wait seemed like forever. His introspection was relentless. Like a hawk, Timmy watched the door of the principal's office.

Then, to Timmy's shock, in walked his father! His father *never* came to the school. What was *he* doing here? This must be really bad.

But his father got down on one knee, took his son's hand, looked into his eyes, and said, "Timmy, I was impatient with you this morning. I'm sorry for yelling. Will you forgive me?"

Stunned, relieved, and not sure how to respond, Timmy gulped, "Sure, Dad!"

Twenty-three years later, Tim shared this story at his father's sixty-fifth birthday party.

As the family sat around, the son hilariously recounted the mischief he and his sister had caused that memorable morning. We were all laughing. But then Tim got serious. He recounted the moment when his father asked for his forgiveness. He described it as though it had been yesterday and said, "That event was one of the most influential in my life. When I do something stupid and lose my cool, I remember that day. It even influences the way I treat my wife."

The great lessons of life are seldom planned. They are not prepared or given as lectures. They are seldom taught in the classroom. Those memories that are seared into our consciences and impact our actions happen when we least expect them—when we give flesh to our faith.

We never know how our actions will influence others. When Roger asked forgiveness from his young son, he was not trying to teach him a "life lesson." Roger was exercising contrition. Roger's conscience told him that he had acted inappropriately toward a fellow human being. It did not matter if the person he harmed was sixty or six, a politician or a child. Roger confessed his wrongdoing in an act of contrition. As often happens, this act of contrition became a living sermon that would never be forgotten. When was the last time you went out of your way to seek forgiveness?

A Gift of Contrition

I remember something one of my priest friends had said once, that grace is having a commitment to—or at least an acceptance of—being ineffective and foolish. That our bottled charm is the main roadblock to drinking that clear cool glass of love.

Anne Lamott

"This morning we are going to take communion," announced Darcy. It was Monday morning staff meeting time, and everyone had gathered for a time of worship and announcements. Darcy had requested to lead the session. "We're about to break for Christmas, and I thought it might be good to clear the air and do some reconciliation."

Since I was sitting in the front row, I could not see the faces of those behind me. But my intuitive antennae picked up the discomfort of our staff sitting in rows two, three, and four. I heard a chair push back against the carpet and footsteps heading to the back of the auditorium. One person had bolted for the door in an act of protest.

"We're not going to take communion in the traditional sense," Darcy continued. I could feel my body tightening. I knew I should have previewed her material. But it was too late. "I invite you to come up, take the bread and the wine, and serve it to someone in the group." Darcy pinched off some bread, dipped it in the wine, and walked to a young man in the second row. She got down on one knee and lifted the elements toward him. By this time all thirty staff members were mesmerized, holding their breath.

It had been a tough, busy month; nerves were frayed, and everyone needed a break. There had been a lot of interstaff conflict. The buzzword in the hallways had been *mistrust*. Promises had been broken. Staff had been let down. Gossip had been swirling. And, of course, at the center of the whirlwind was Darcy. Whether fair or not, the accusations had been flying through our community like darts looking for a target. And now Darcy was extending an olive branch?

"Randy," whispered Darcy loud enough for all to hear, "I violated your trust. I broke your confidence. I'm sorry. Please accept my apology."

Darcy moved to an empty seat and sat down as a few more staff left the room. Fortunately, others moved toward the table at the front of the room and began serving one another bread and wine.

I do not know what was said in the other staff exchanges. I just hoped they were words of encouragement, apology, and reconciliation—words to clear the air, forgive, and move forward.

Sadly, some staff refused to participate; they thought Darcy was just being manipulative. She had no business calling for contrition—at Christmas, of all times!

I had to admire her courage to ask for forgiveness from a brother in front of the whole group. "Oh, she should have done that in private," people whispered. "She didn't need to bring the whole group into her business."

But I was not so sure, especially in the context of our close-knit community where everybody's business turns out to be everybody's business. A number of the issues pertaining to the conflict had been discussed—well, gossiped about—with many in the group. But wisely or otherwise, Darcy wanted to get it all out in the open.

Our Christmas display of public contrition raised perplexing questions about forgiveness and the role our motives play in seeking forgiveness. Did Darcy have any right to ask forgiveness *publicly*? Did she have manipulative motives? Was she using the event to impress her boss? Was she just trying to cover up mistakes she had made? Fair questions.

Those questions evoke others: As Christians, do we have the right to refuse someone's apology based on our judgment of their motives? Didn't Jesus say something about forgiving our brother or sister 7 times—or how about 490 times? Isn't it true that by the hundredth act of forgiving, most of us would doubt the offender's sincerity? "Oh, come on, is he for real? If he were really sorry, he'd do something about his behavior!"

But Jesus does not seem to give us the authority to judge another's motives. The real issue behind our inability to receive another person's request for forgiveness is our insatiable demand for justice (revenge, actually) that we feel should precede the act of forgiveness. Strangely, our forgiveness only seems to become easier *after* we feel justice has been served. Once the offending brother or sister has *earned* our forgiveness—jumped through the necessary hoops and paid the necessary penalties, if not embarrassments—then we *may* extend our grace.

The book of Acts reminds me that Paul's transformation was not the result of strict justice demanded by the one (Christ) who had been hurt by Paul's persecution. Theologian Miroslav Volf writes that the exalted Christ, in his self-identification with the church, was the victim of Paul's zeal and his supposed religious cleansing. Every time one of Jesus's followers was persecuted by Paul, Jesus was hurt. So the resurrected Lord shouted, "Saul! Saul! Why are you persecuting *me?*" (Acts 9:4 NLT, emphasis added). God's grace stunningly met Paul in a dramatic form when Paul was on his way to Damascus. According to Volf, it is compelling that Jesus did not exact justice *before* grace was extended to Paul.[6] Counterintuitively, no retribution was demanded of Paul for his past sins. No penance or "doing time" was extracted before God's loving hand was extended. God's movement toward Paul was not conditional upon any kind of altered behavior.

Provocative questions are evoked by the Damascus encounter: Would Paul ever have become an apostle if Jesus had demanded some form of retribution, some form of justice, before the extension of grace? Would Paul have written so boldly about grace and God's love had he not experienced it in such a powerful and personal way? We will never know. But we do know that Paul's future was dedicated to teaching about the mystery of God's grace.

Although Paul was stunningly and dramatically confronted about his behavior and reprimanded, peace between Paul and Jesus was not the result of *justice*. Rather, peace between Paul and Jesus was the result of an act of *undeserved grace*.

And this is the very gospel that today still gets under our fingernails, makes us perspire, creates discomfort, and ultimately reveals the condition of our hearts. It takes courage to acknowledge and confess our wrongs. That's why Jesus was pleased with Darcy's courage, even if it may have been tinted with impure motives and executed in a fashion that did not suit everyone's fancy. It also takes tremendous courage, and a heart full of grace, for any of us to forgive and embrace the one who has wronged us.

For many of us, the model guiding our view of forgiveness is based on the theory of retribution. For example, if a person commits a wrong against me, that person must somehow "pay" for what he or she has done. This idea can take different forms. In our sophisticated and politically correct culture, our desire for justice is not always overt and obvious. Maybe I refuse to accept the person's apology—and then I, justifying it by my moral high ground, spread mean rumors about him or her. Or maybe I refuse to allow the individual to reenter our social community by failing to invite the person to certain events and activities. Sure, I may verbally accept his or her apology. But my actions do not really reflect forgiveness. The questions we must grapple with are: How do we respond to a person who hurts us and then seeks our forgiveness? Do we have the right to doubt that person's motives and refuse his or her attempts at reconciliation?

Letting Go of Our Little Lives

A prophet's task is to reveal the fault lines hidden beneath the comfortable surface of the worlds we invent for ourselves, the national myths as well as the little lies and delusions of control and security that get us through the day.

Kathleen Norris, *The Cloister Walk*

"May I borrow your key to get into the supply closet?" asked Julie Green, our young, vivacious second-grade teacher. Ms. Gil had just locked the resource closet and was returning to her classroom.

"You'll have to get a key from the administrative office," Ms. Gil said with a dismissive squaring of her shoulders. "You should know the policy by now."

"But you're standing right here," Julie said, bewildered by the absurdity of Ms. Gil's position.

"Policy is policy. You know the rules."

The supply closet sits at the end of a hallway, just outside the first-grade classroom. Only two keys to the closet exist. One hangs somewhere in the principal's office; Ms. Gil possesses the other. It's not clear how she came to have her own personal key, but it was probably just by default because she was the most senior teacher—the only teacher to outlast every administrative transition the school had seen. No one really cared that she had a key—until today.

Now Julie went into overdrive. Until now she had bitten her tongue in staff meetings just to keep the peace, but this was too much. Somebody had to stand up to the unreasonable Ms. Gil. Having seniority didn't give her the right to be thoughtless and absurd. Julie's face was red with rage. "You're the reason why so many of us are thinking of leaving the school," barked Julie. "You're the reason morale is so low on staff. Everybody just bows down to you and lets you get away with this kind of stuff. Your behavior shouldn't be tolerated!" She stormed off.

I received a memo from Miss Green confessing her intemperate behavior, but she also reminded administration that we had a real problem. "I'm not the only teacher who has difficulty working with—or rather, *around*—her."

Fortunately, our principal sees conflict as an opportunity for spiritual and personal growth and a chance to put faith into action. One of her famous aphorisms is, "There will always be conflict, but it is how one handles it that makes the difference."

The next week our principal took Roberta Gil, her embattled teacher, to dinner. They talked about the weather, the kids, movies, and then finally the incident that had taken place the previous week. Roberta was receptive to the wise counsel of her supervisor but still had difficulty understanding why her colleague was such a pain.

"I have an idea: why don't you just wrap up the key," said the wise principal, "and give it away? You know, put it in a little box, wrap it in colorful paper, put a bow on it, and just hand it to Julie." The idea had never crossed Ms. Gil's mind because she *enjoyed* having the only key. In her soul she cherished the fact that she had something that no one else possessed. It gave her a little (just a *little*, mind you) more power, a control that the other teachers didn't have. So why let go of the key?

"If you *really* want to grow as a child of God," our principal gently suggested, "you've got to quit hanging on so tightly to *little things*." Then she slid her tightly clenched fist across the table. "Right now this is you. Your fist is a symbol of your heart—it's closed." Slowly she began to peel her fingers back one by one until her palm was fully open. "This is the way God wants us to be. Open. Loosely, gently, graciously holding the things we possess."

The dramatic image touched Ms. Gil. Her key, a precious key wrapped in a small box and given away, would be more than just a token gift. It would be a symbol of a deeper spiritual truth—the act would represent a kind of self-giving, a death of sorts.

Imagine the reaction of the faculty as they witnessed Roberta Gil's change in attitude. Something wonderful would occur through her act of reconciliation.

Most of us, if we are completely honest, are carbon copies of Roberta Gil. We may not guard school supply closets, but we all clasp *our* keys and guard *our* things that do not really matter in the eternal scheme. We wrap our fingers around tiny, inconsequential trivia, guarding it at all costs. We wield our stuttering expressions of power, never realizing that we thereby sacrifice the presence of God. We settle for defending supply closets when God wants to remake us into a refreshing creation—a geyser of life flowing with love, compassion, and grace; a person whose image of self is not withered and grasping to one-up our peers. We should be people with open hands, open hearts, and open minds.

J. R. R. Tolkien's Lord of the Rings has a wonderful theme that reminds us of the diminishing returns of power. Remember the story? Everybody wanted to possess a very special magical ring. They wanted to possess the ring because it gave power. There was just one problem: the tighter anyone held on to the ring, the more that person's humanity became diminished. Concern for others was replaced with selfishness. Noble intentions gave way to greed. Love turned to hate. Bonds of friendship were broken. Hearts were hardened. Unabated power turned out to lead to the rotting of the soul and the eventual destruction of the individual. The only person in the story who could handle the ring was the person who did not want it. Frodo, the unassuming hobbit, was selected to carry the ring simply because his character did not have the need to lord it over others.

As I read the Gospel accounts of Jesus, I am struck by the pattern of self-emptying in his life. He avoided every opportunity to build status. He did not exploit his ability to heal. Spending time with powerful people was not the way he envisioned fulfilling his mission. He renounced accumulating "stuff," worldly possessions. He refused to turn stones into bread. Jesus did not clutch and grasp at the things of this world. He truly lived out his teaching that "where your treasure is, there your heart will be also" (Matt. 6:21).

J. Heinrich Arnold claims, "What a great gift it would be if we could see a little of the great vision of Jesus—if we could see beyond our small lives! Certainly our view is very limited. But we can at least ask him to call us out of our small worlds and our self-centeredness, and we can at least ask to feel the challenge of the great harvest that must be gathered."[7]

May we all begin to see the great vision of Jesus and let go of inconsequential keys that keep our hearts pinched and our visions out of focus. May we "feel the challenge of the great harvest" that is waiting to be gathered.

What are the "keys" you desperately clutch, consequently forfeiting the larger gifts God wants to give you? If you are like me, those "keys" can be titles or positions that provide me with certain amounts of power. They can be material and symbolic things, such as cars, zip codes, or brand-name clothing that get people to look at me in a different way. I must remember that the tighter I clutch these *things*, the smaller my life becomes. The story of Ms. Gil challenges me to reassess the things I hold so dearly—especially when those tiny expressions of power are used to exalt myself above other people. Acting contritely is the only way to break the control these things have over me and open my heart to experiencing more of God in my life.

The Blessing of Imperfection

The reason why people are not open in communications is the fear of being judged and evaluated.

Carl Rogers

The event was billed as a "Men on a Mission Dinner." But it turned out to be a classic church dinner—where everyone sits on metal chairs in a drafty gymnasium and eats fried chicken, mashed potatoes, and green beans. The table talk was about who would win the Super Bowl and the next church workday project. The portable PA system didn't quite work and sounded like a nine-dollar walkie-talkie. I felt sorry for the emcee when he tried to tell a joke. No one understood it. No one laughed.

I was the featured speaker and was supposed to talk about manhood and God. Since the boundaries of the assigned topic were as broad as the Mississippi, permitting me to talk about almost anything, I decided to skip the athletic metaphors and Old Testament stories of heroic men and try something a little more daring. I brought a couple of guests who worked with me in our ministry to do a talk show format.

161

I had invited Tom, who was around fifty-five years old, a late-in-life convert to Christianity who had tried about every other religion before coming to faith. Subsequently, he decided to give a couple of years to missionary service. A carpenter by trade, Tom brought his much-needed gifts to our inner-city mission. He could fix and repair anything. Along the way he ended up mentoring my other guest, Sugar Will.

Sugar Will and Tom were not at all alike. Tom grew up in the sixties, listened to the Beatles and the Grateful Dead, and had never spent any time in the inner city. Sugar Will was a son of the inner city, thirty years Tom's junior, who loved rap music and knew nothing outside his neighborhood. But the two connected. They played pool together, went to the movies, and stayed up late to talk about life and faith. Tom helped Sugar Will get his life on track—he was the father who cared, just what Sugar Will needed.

I positioned the two onstage and began to fire questions at them. My hope was for the audience to catch a glimpse of how an older man can mentor and make a significant difference in the life of a younger man. After a few questions of introduction that helped everyone feel more comfortable, I began to dig a little deeper.

"Sugar Will," I prodded, "what's Tom really like?"

For a moment Sugar Will paused and looked at the audience, then said, "Well, he doesn't pretend to be perfect like other Christians. I guess it's because he's made mistakes."

The audience erupted in laughter. Tom turned a few shades of red, and I was caught a little off guard. After all, this was a church function, and I wasn't sure what kinds of mistakes Tom had shared with his young friend. I knew Tom's past had been pretty colorful. And Sugar Will was unaware of the unspoken rules of church. He wouldn't know how to candy coat his statements. But on impulse I decided to continue. "What do you mean, 'He's not perfect like other Christians'?"

"Well," he started, hesitated, then said abruptly, "most Christians I know walk around like they never done nothin' bad. Like they're perfect—or tryin' to be perfect. But I can talk to Tom, 'cause he's done bad stuff too."

I am not sure what others in the audience heard that night, but Sugar Will's comments pierced me like an arrow. Without intent or malice, Sugar Will indicted most of Christendom— those earnest, terribly pious Christians who inadvertently can be spiritual roadblocks to kids like Sugar Will. Those sincere Christians project a sense of perfection and communicate an alienating message: "I've got it all together. How about you?"

However, for young men and women who are disengaged from things of God and don't have it all together, the perception of perfect Christians creates a wall between themselves and the God who may have something to offer. Sugar Will could never open up, never be vulnerable with them or share his struggles, because people whom he perceived to be perfect were also people whom he would feel judged by.

This dilemma is not unique to the inner city. A recent study suggests that many young people go to the Internet rather than to church for their spiritual nourishment. These young seekers anonymously visit chat rooms and engage in dialogue with other seekers. Why? Because they can be honest without being judged. They can share their struggles and doubts without a sense of condemnation. Yet this generation wants a place where they can be honest and can find acceptance for who they are and where they are in life. Sadly, too often the church is not the place where these young people can turn.

One of the wonderful characteristics of the Bible—probably the thing that makes it most believable—is that it does not project perfect people as examples of godliness. The Bible is pretty vulnerable. One would think that the writers would have gone to greater efforts to make their heroes, well, a little more heroic. But Moses is presented as a fearful, often doubt-filled leader. David abuses his power, seduces a woman, and

163

then tries to cover it up with murder. Jonah prays for God's wrath on those he has just converted. Samson? Well, there was Delilah. Solomon made a good start but took a few wrong turns. The disciples? They were far from being the A-Team, whether it was Peter putting his foot in his mouth and denying Christ or James and John completely missing the message of Jesus. The disciples are not portrayed as moral and intellectual superstars. In short, the Bible seems to be an account of flawed men and women who are embraced by God's grace and used for God's remarkable purposes.

Furthermore, one of the most intriguing aspects of Jesus seen in the Gospels is his approachability. Whether it was people who had stolen from and cheated others, women who had sold their bodies for sexual pleasures, people with hideous diseases, children, or those banished from the religious "in crowd," people approached Jesus. Unlike pious religious leaders who kept people at a distance, Jesus's godliness was an invitation for those who did not have it all together. He wanted them to come and find healing and life.

Perhaps one of the other reasons people were drawn to Jesus was that he did not make a big show of his religious activities. He was genuine and without pretense, not focused on what other people thought of him—especially those in positions of religious power. His lifestyle was not just a legalistic adherence to a set of behaviors so that he could have acceptance from the holy people of his day. Quite the contrary—Jesus seemed to be doing the wrong things in the eyes of those who thought they were perfect.

How important it is for those who are broken, struggling, and in fear of condemnation to meet faith-filled people who have discarded their pretensions of perfection, have dropped their masks of having it all together, and are willing to show the world a broken and contrite heart. The church needs more people like my friends Tom and Sugar Will—those who truly embrace God's relentless, unearned grace and as a result of that grace are not afraid to let the world see that they too are imperfect and human.

That night's banquet ended after another forty minutes of dialogue. Sugar Will showed all his magnificent smile. Tom gave us both a huge bear hug. All those who had attended agreed they needed a more authentic sense of themselves and their commitment to Christ.

The church does not need people who spend their whole lives trying to project a public image of perfection. The church needs people who are honest—honest with their struggles, honest with their doubts, and honest with their pasts. People who can embody this spirit of contrition, the ability to confess shortcomings and imperfections, are people who truly understand God's grace and forgiveness. These are the kind of people that broken people need to meet: people who are able to relax and live in the assurance that God's grace is truly sufficient. In what ways can you be more vulnerable? Do you find yourself always trying to project an image of perfection?

Brains in the Way

I want to simplify your lives. When others are telling you to read more, I want to tell you to read less; when others are telling you to do more, I want to tell you to do less. The world does not need more of you; it needs more of God. Your friends do not need more of you; they need more of God. And you don't need more of you; you need more of God.

Eugene H. Peterson

John took a sip of his coffee, then placed his Starbucks mug on the table, looked at me with a note of seriousness, and said, "It's hard to believe, but egos really get in the way—especially with highly intelligent people. Pride is blinding. It's really true."

John was a successful venture capitalist who had used his background in mathematics to gain success in the commodities market. The mathematical formula his company created had helped his company become extremely profitable. And, surprisingly and happily, before John turned forty, his company was sold to a large Swiss bank. Now John can spend a great deal of his time volunteering with different service ministries.

During our meeting he began to muse about human nature. "When my company was just getting off the ground, I hired a brilliant physicist from Germany. At age twelve—yes, twelve—that boy had won the German National Math Contest. That guy was bright. I mean *really* bright!" John chuckled and continued, "That guy created a formula and thought the company should implement his idea right away. But I knew his idea was wrong, and I knew it wouldn't work on the market."

"How did he respond to your critique?" I asked.

"Can you believe he yelled at me, 'What do you mean it won't work?' And then he screamed and slammed his fist on the table. He was not even remotely open to the idea that his formula might not yield the kinds of profits we were used to."

"So how'd you handle it?"

"Well, he just wouldn't listen to me. He was very persistent for a young man. So I gave him a little money and said, 'Okay, use your formula for a year, and then we'll talk.' Sure enough, a year later he had lost all the money. You know what?" John mused. "He still wouldn't listen. Now that's arrogance!"

John's story was so intriguing that I decided to share it with a friend, a lawyer named Jay. In twenty years in the legal profession, Jay had seen many attorneys come and go. When I told him about John's former employee, he said, "You know, Bruce, the same thing is true in my field. The better the lawyer, the more they confess to *not* knowing. They spend considerable time looking at things from different perspectives. But there are," he said with a knowing smile, "a lot of lawyers who are just too arrogant to consider another point of view. They're usually the lousy lawyers."

After I heard these two accounts, I had to do some soul searching of my own. I had to ask the question, in what ways are pride and arrogance blinding me from seeing truth? Are there people I am not listening to because I think I have a corner on truth? Are there agendas and ideas that I need to look at from another perspective? Pride and arrogance can blind us. None of us is beyond this temptation, especially when it comes to matters of faith. After all, the Pharisees had all the right answers, but they missed the larger truth that Jesus was trying to teach. Their arrogance and pride hardened their hearts. Their insistence that they knew the truth blinded them from considering the message of Jesus.

Without a doubt the toughest aspect of our Christian faith is getting our egos under control. That's probably why the great Christian apologist C. S. Lewis argued, "The essential vice, the utmost evil, is pride. Unchastity, anger, greed, drunkenness, and all that are mere flea-bites in comparison: it was through pride that the devil became the devil; pride leads to every other vice; it is the complete anti-God state of mind."[8] Too often we find our identity and our sense of worth in *our* ideas and the things we have accomplished. Laying down our lives, our ideas, our preconceived notions, our perceptions, and our stereotypes is always a difficult task. It involves embracing the idea that we may not always be right—that there is much that we do not know and much that we need to learn.

As I mentioned earlier in this book, one of our great faith traditions is *The Rule of Saint Benedict*. Saint Benedict was a monk who created *The Rule of Saint Benedict*—a set of guidelines developed in the sixth century to help people grow in their spiritual lives. Many principles make up *The Rule of Benedict*, but it is interesting that at the center of the Benedictine order is the discipline of *humility*. Saint Benedict believed that all spirituality was built around the ability

167

to cultivate a spirit of humility. He likened humility to the beautiful courtyard in his monastery—a place filled with light, flowers, and plants. And as it was the center of the monastery, the courtyard permeated the rest of the monastery with a sense of peace, tranquility, and beauty.

As the center of his monastery was the courtyard, Saint Benedict believed that *humility* needed to become the center of our spiritual lives. Without humility, nothing else is right. Thus excessive pride must be broken. Benedict believed that the pride needing to be broken was the insistent desire to be our own god, or to control other people or other things. He said that instead, we must let God be God. So often, Benedict believed, we make other things in life our little gods—our jobs, our ideas, our things, our titles. Consequently, we eventually forget who God really is. And when we forget the reality of God, we tend to become the center of our universe and lose our humility.

Joan Chittister reminds us what it means to be truly humble when she writes: "People who are really humble, who know themselves to be *earth* or *humus*—the root from which our word 'humble' comes—have about themselves an air of self-containment and self-control. There's no haughtiness, no distance, no sarcasm, no put downs, no airs or importance or disdain."[9] Embracing a healthy understanding of our position in the creation of the world can be important for keeping a healthy perspective on ourselves in relation to both God and people.

The apostle Paul also builds on this theme of humility as he instructs the church of Philippi to "do nothing out of selfish ambition or vain conceit, but in humility consider others better than yourselves" (Phil. 2:3). Now those are words to live by! They are words to guide all our interactions with other people.

Living contritely involves humility. It takes humility to say "I'm sorry." It takes humility to admit that we were wrong. It takes humility to listen empathically to another person. It takes humility to see life from another perspective. It takes humility to repair past wrongs. But acts of contrition and confession have the capacity to break the stronghold of pride that prevents us from living with humility. How might you live more contritely? Are there past wrongs you need to make right?

> Lord,
> there is nothing more difficult than saying, "I'm
>   sorry."
> My instinct for preserving facades of perfection re-
>   sists costly confession.
> I am sorry for those times I justify my wrong actions
>   with lies to others and myself.
> My desire is to taste your salvation—freedom from
>   forces rotting away the abundant life you promise.
> I pray for the audacious nerve to cut the tentacles
>   of self-deception by returning the life stolen from
>   others—
> whether in my words or deeds—fourfold!
> Amen.

9

FAITH NOTICED

When Jesus saw their faith . . .
Matthew 9:2

Prayer was the furthest thing from my mind.

Even on a good day, prayer doesn't come easily for me. It's always a struggle. Thirty-second prayers are doable: driving to work in the morning, I say, "Lord, help me to be a blessing to others today," or "Lord, watch over my family." But focused times of extended prayer are a challenge as my to-do list interrupts my petitions and praises, enticing me down paths at odds with divine communion.

To add to my dismay, I have long admired those pious fathers and mothers of church history who always seemed able to block out the world and commune with God for hours. Their devotion to solitude and quiet contemplation and their ability to renounce the cares of this world challenge me to move beyond a laundry list of supplications and meditate

171

beyond my mere surface prayers. Unfortunately, for me *desire* and *self-discipline* are not always the best of friends.

One particular day fourteen years ago, I was so emotionally frantic that even a "Help me, God!" wasn't possible.

Instead, I was assaulted by a whirlwind of doctors' meetings, emergency room vigils, and alarming medical reports suggesting that our situation was getting worse. God's presence was elusive; rather, dread was hanging over me like a dark cloud, blocking even the faintest ray of hope.

Certainly, I had not lost my faith in God. Nor was I blaming God for what was happening. My theological bent favors the belief that God's great gift to humanity is our freedom to make good and bad choices. Therefore, I embrace the reality that bad things do happen and my being a Christian does not guarantee a special divine force field deflecting hardship away from me. Everyone's experience can be fraught with danger, disease, and disappointment—that's life. Being human is a difficult, risky enterprise. So shaking a fist at God and crying, "Why me?" does not fit with my belief. But that day I just couldn't pray in the surreal world that I had been thrust into—a life that revolved around a five-hundred-square-foot neonatal emergency room full of premature babies, with white-clad doctors solemnly rotating in and out. Plucked out of my familiar comforts, I was trying to regain my bearings in a sterile, colorless room with flashing lights and uncomfortable waiting room chairs. Gone were the comforts of my bed, my morning paper, and my desk. Gone was the predictability of an eight-hour workday and dinner with my wife and son. I was now trying to make sense of the fact that my newborn daughter was about to die. I was powerless. *There was nothing I could do!*

Oh, the baby's first trimester had passed without any special trips to a gynecologist; morning sickness for Pamela had been minimal. Early signs indicated this was to be a normal pregnancy. Then I received an emergency phone call in New

Jersey in the early evening hours of a hot July day and was told to be at the emergency room of Georgetown University Hospital in Washington right away. Needless to say, at that moment my life took a dramatic change. Pam, who had been caring for her eighty-year-old grandmother in Arlington, had surprisingly discovered that she had a ruptured placenta, and our baby's premature delivery was imminent.

Four days after Pam's water broke, our one-pound daughter was delivered. With legs like matchsticks and tubes taped to a Barbie doll–sized head, baby Erin was little more than a wisp of human life. She was shrouded in a small incubator with heat lamps, vaporizers, and purifiers. Images of snuggling with a healthy newborn were dashed. There would be no holding, no cuddling, and no pictures. We could only peer through the separating glass from a distance.

Urgent decisions had to be made about heart surgery or using a new respiratory drug to strengthen her underdeveloped lungs. In the whirlwind of confusion and doctors' advice, we were asked to endorse certain experimental procedures so that doctors and researchers could try out their new techniques on our daughter.

I paced the room and bit my nails in anticipation, waiting for the doctor to burst through the door to pronounce . . . what? Sleep was not possible. Reading, incomprehensible. Talking about the future, not relevant. I decided to write letters to my new daughter who was not to be, trying to capture some of my feelings on paper—hoping beyond hope that she might read them one day. Two days after her birth I wrote:

> Dear Erin . . . When people congratulate me on your birth, it is hard to get real excited. It's a little like getting a beautiful birthday gift and then dreading the possibility that it might be taken away. You are our gift, and we desire to hang on to you, but we fear getting too close or too attached because you might have to leave.

I remember many events of those early days of Erin's life, but what left the deepest impression on me was the faith of friends. Not *my* faith. The faith of our friends and our family—their belief and their hope that our daughter would live and thrive. I wrote on July 31, 1991:

> Dear Erin . . . We have notified everyone we know who prays, and they will be on their knees tonight. Perhaps this is God's blessing to us and our family. Perhaps the blessing of fellowship is that so many hearts can unite together for a common purpose. People are praying for you, Erin! We hope that God will grant you life and health.

A few days later, when Pam and I were physically and emotionally exhausted, three of my co-workers visited the hospital. Anxiety and dread overwhelmed me. Yet their presence was comforting. Even more comforting than their presence was the faith they possessed. As friends who were not paralyzed by the barrage of doctors' briefings and hourly reports on Erin's breathing patterns, they were one step removed from our condition. Because of this distance, they possessed a kind of certitude and confidence. I wrote to Erin:

> Robert, Gina, and Jodina came to visit today. They were deeply moved by your condition. There were tears in their eyes as they peered at your little body in the incubator. . . . They believe so strongly in the power of prayer. Erin, they are praying for you with all their hearts and souls. Their faith and love for you has made my faith and love for you grow. You will be amazed by how other people's lives will affect and shape you in such strange ways. As humans we give to one another through our words and actions.

After their departure I found a few moments to go outside and be warmed by the setting sun. Later I wrote about the moment:

Yesterday, Erin, a strange thing happened. I was very anxious in the morning. I took a walk outside, and I felt somewhat overwhelmed by the love of God. All around me there was an overpowering sensation that God loved me and was very near to me. I had never felt anything quite so strong. I had an indescribable peace that things were going to work out for you.

I am not sure what happened during the visit from our three friends. But there was a sense of calm after they left. They had brought the gift of hope and their faith that good things could happen. Possibility reflected from their eyes. In the wake of their encounter was a wave of peace. *Their* faith, not mine, bolstered me in that moment.

How does God work in these situations? Why are some people healed while others aren't? It is still a mystery. But I know two things: one, the faith of friends can carry us when our own faith wanes; and two, my daughter is about to turn fourteen as I write this! She is healthy, beautiful, and the most spiritually sensitive of our children.

The faith of our friends made the difference.

WHAT IS FAITH?

Draw me a picture of faith. If I asked you to, what would you draw? What image would you use? What colors would you select? If you are like me, this might be a difficult task. Faith is difficult to draw or paint. Even words are limited in defining this frequently used idea. The words selected by the writer of Hebrews to describe faith are beautiful—"Faith is the assurance of things hoped for, the conviction of things not seen" (Heb. 11:1 NRSV)—but they are still a little lofty and esoteric. What constitutes "things hoped for"? What limitations do we need to place on the notion of "things not seen"?

When reading the teachings of Jesus, it is interesting to note how little Jesus talked in the abstract. Instead of trying to wordsmith the idea of faith and provide a wordy definition for his listeners, Jesus chose to *notice* expressions of faith in the midst of an ordinary day and affirm them. When Jesus noticed these acts of living faith, he called his listeners to take note. By teaching in this manner, Jesus left his followers memorable images of what it meant to exercise faith.

The story of Jesus healing a paralyzed man in Matthew 9 provides one of those images that is hard to dismiss or forget. In this passage Matthew shares few details about the paralytic, other than that he had a debilitating disease—and a few good friends, an important element in the story that cannot be overlooked. Imagine having friends take a day off work, carry you across town on a stretcher, push their way through a crowd, and get you up-close-and-personal time with the most remarkable man of the day. This says a lot about the commitment and love of this man's friends. They obviously cared a great deal. They wanted to see their friend healed. They believed Jesus could do something. *They* had faith!

Since Matthew makes no mention of the paralytic's faith in this story, one could wonder if the unidentified man had any faith, even had a kernel of belief that he could be healed. Year after year of lying on his back, being severely restricted in his mobility, would surely have diminished his aptitude to believe that he could experience any kind of healing. As he tried and failed to straighten his twisted hands year after year, surely it would have been impossible for him to envision holding his own drinking cup. As he attempted to balance himself on his two legs, only to fall face-first into the dirt, he surely would have laughed at the prospect of walking. These were not the days of rehab centers, physical therapists, and nerve surgery. If someone was born a paralytic, he remained a paralytic. So naturally the man had come to the point of accepting the condition of his body. He would always be dependent on other people.

But the broken man's faith did not seem to matter. And Jesus said it was the faith of *his friends* that brought about the healing. The startling picture that Jesus leaves for his listeners is one of four faithful friends who had rolled up their sleeves and expressed their love and devotion for a friend by bearing his stretcher. The friends moved forward with a collective faith, believing that Jesus could and would heal.

CONTEMPLATING FAITH

I have often heard people say, as I'm sure you have too, "If I could only experience a miracle, then I would believe; then I would have faith." This, of course, seldom is true, nor is it consistent with the gospel message. The theme that resurfaces repeatedly in the Gospels is that the act of faith generally *precedes* the miracle. A person initiates a movement toward Jesus in faith and then experiences the miracle. Miracles do not create faith. Faith, expressed in action, creates miracles.

One of the most vivid examples of this principle is found in Mark 8. Jesus had just fed five thousand people, cast a demon out of a young girl, engaged in a heavy theological discussion with the Pharisees, healed a crippled and mute man, and fed another four thousand people. A busy week—even for Jesus.

Then the disciples got on a boat with Jesus. They had only brought one loaf of bread and were concerned about not having enough food for dinner. At that point Jesus confronted them and said, "Are your hearts hardened? Do you have eyes but fail to see, and ears but fail to hear?" (Mark 8:17–18). Let me loosely translate Jesus's words to his disciples: "What else do I need to do to get your attention?" (Or as we might say today, "You knuckleheads!") Mark apparently wants us to see that the observation of miracles and wonders has little impact on the depths of our faith.

Faith is not the by-product of a miracle or of a sure affirmation of doctrine. Faith is an attitude, a behavior that creates conditions in which miracles can occur. Faith is the water that primes the pump. It is the spadework that prepares the garden for planting. Faith creates the environment in which miracles can occur.

So Jesus affirmed the action of the four men who had yet to experience a miracle for their paralyzed friend. Why then did Jesus call their activity *faith*? I believe it was the hope they embodied in the arduous task of scheming, lifting their friend, and delivering him to Jesus. It was faith because there was no guarantee that anything would result from their actions. Their faith-filled activity was what created the opportunity for a miracle to occur.

Peter J. Gomes, the minister of Harvard University's Memorial Church, heard a sermon based on this passage of Scripture when he was a seminary student at Harvard. The sermon was delivered by a Mennonite professor of theology named Gordon D. Kaufman. Gomes recalled, "The point the professor was trying to make was that our faith may make a difference for good in the life of someone else. Had the friends simply believed that Jesus could heal, had they just hoped for the healing of their friend, nothing would have happened; but they acted upon their convictions, translated their faith into deeds, and made real the vision."[1]

Perhaps that was why Jesus noticed *acts of* faith. Jesus wanted his disciples to see that faith was not something to be hoarded or selfishly enjoyed. Nor was faith something to just sit on like a comfortable chair. If we have been blessed with the belief that God is actively involved in the workings of this world, even if our faith is fleeting and momentary, we must use this faith to benefit other people. Our hope, and our ability to act in that hope, must carry those who are crippled by unbelief to the feet of the God who can transform lives.

Like the four friends of the paralyzed man, we bear the stretchers of those unable to get to a place where God can meet them. And it is the kind of faith Jesus wants us to notice, to embrace, and to exercise.

STORIES OF FAITH NOTICED

The term *faith* has many meanings. Some people associate the term *faith* with the affirmation of certain doctrines. For other people the idea of faith is about believing that God can do certain things, like heal someone. Others see faith as the way people act out their beliefs in the world. So what does Jesus call faith? Frequently throughout the Gospels, we meet a Jesus who affirms ordinary people who take risks in the belief that he can do something special for them. Whether it is a woman who touches Jesus's garment in the belief that he can heal her, a tenacious mother who thinks he can heal her sick daughter and refuses to be turned away, or four guys who carry their friend across town, Jesus affirms the *actions* of these individuals as *faith*. I believe these multiple expressions of faith are acted out by people in our midst today. We need to take note of these acts. Through the examples of these people, we are challenged to live as people of faith.

The Coupon Woman

Stories make us more alive, more human, more courageous, more loving. Why does anybody tell a story? It does indeed have something to do with faith, faith that the universe has meaning, that our little human lives are not irrelevant, that what we choose or say or do matters, matters cosmically.

Madeleine L'Engle, *The Writer*

It was five minutes before 11:00 a.m. on a Sunday. Mauve-and-gold sanctuary windows enhanced the reverent prelude now humming in the background. This was not the time nor the place for running, jumping, and shouting. They knew

179

that. But it was going to happen anyway. I had a fleeting second to corral the dozen kids under my supervision before the reveries of the silver-haired ladies who had come to worship were irrevocably pushed aside for the morning.

At that moment someone grabbed my arm. I knew those fingers—they belonged to frail, seventy-year-old Gladys. She defied her arthritis and paid no notice to her stained dresses. "I've got something for you, Reverend," she stage-whispered. Letting go of my arm, she dug through the hankies, breath mints, and keys in her black plastic purse. She retrieved a crumpled three-by-six envelope.

Week after week Gladys brought me these little gifts. I wasn't interested at this particular moment. I didn't have time. I was annoyed. The kids were about to explode, un-supervised, on the congregation that sat contemplating the beatific vision. Gladys placed the envelope in my hand. It had my wife's name on it, so I stuffed it in my pocket and begged off, chasing up the aisle after my charges. I would save the day, little realizing that in the tyranny of the urgent, I was about to miss the moment.

A few days later, while rummaging through my coat pocket, I pulled out the envelope and two others from previous weeks. I was more than annoyed. Coupons. Ten, twenty, fifty of them. In my youthful impatience I questioned, "Who has time to clip coupons?" Pampers, Huggies, Gerber baby food, wipes—name any baby product! Each of the clipped-together coupons was neatly cut, each shouting the incredible bargain and better life available through its use. Worse, I already had a stack of those annoyances cluttering my desk.

I pitched them in the trash. They were of no value to me.

Gladys! I suddenly thought as they thunked in the basket. Each coupon had taken time to meticulously cut. Each represented a thought for my son who would need Pampers, a thought about my wife who could save a few cents on baby food. This annoying elderly lady was thinking about *my* family. Each time Gladys pulled her scissors from her sewing kit, she had thought about a need my family had. Like an old nun praying her rosary day after day, faithfully remembering and meditating on a list of people and needs, Gladys thought of *our* family. I was sure that each clip began with a smile, perhaps a simple prayer for our children. Not once, not twice, but thirty or forty times a week. As Gladys read her newspaper, she thought of us. As Gladys waded through junk mail, she had my children in mind. In the most mundane event of Gladys's life, she thought about *me*.

I, on the other hand, saw no value in the coupons. I was busy quieting rambunctious kids, "doing the work of the Lord." I never paused to reflect that if each kind thought about a person is like a prayer, then these coupons were golden. In the sea of excess, in the flood of unwanted paper and commercial bombardment, those clippings were drawing an old woman to care for me and my household.

I retrieved them. They were not junk. They were sacramental reminders.

I now have little coupons posted around our house in places I look most often. At the refrigerator I am reminded by coupons to pray for and think of others. At the bathroom mirror I think of another person, another family, another need. I am trying to be as faithful as frail Gladys, who interrupts my life each Sunday with her predictable, extraordinarily thoughtful gift.

One day when I meet the Maker, look back over my life, and have a chance to see what prayers and thoughts from others averted disaster from my household, my hunch is, I will be shown thousands of coupons that represent innumerable prayers on behalf of me and my family.

Praying takes faith. It takes faith to enter into God's presence each day on behalf of other people, believing that God hears you and will respond in some way to your request. I am humbled by people like Gladys—people who anonymously think beyond themselves and petition God to watch over me and my family. In a world that seems so bent on serving itself, the action of Gladys is revolutionary. Gladys is a model of faith I need to emulate. Do you ever engage in the selfless act of praying for another person? This might be a good way to begin to cultivate the practice of faith in your life.

It Has Been over Thirty Years

Jesus' teachings are not mere suggestions, but pointed challenges to grow. They state urgently, baldly, and sometimes harshly what the "path to life" really is. They are not ideals, but the Ultimate Practicality. They are statements of the necessary conditions for the flowering of the deepest human capacities, the growth of the *imago Dei*.

Robert Morris

I admire the late Mother Teresa of Calcutta. I have read articles and watched the documentaries chronicling her committed service to broken people. Her work with the poor and dying in Calcutta was exemplary, as are her collected words and sayings that have made her one of the more "quotable" people of the twentieth century.

In my admiration I assumed that this tiny, frail Albanian woman—a modern-day icon of sacrifice, commitment, and compassion—always felt enveloped by the Spirit of God. I assumed she was transfixed by God's presence as she took the Eucharist each morning. I felt certain she felt mystically connected to Jesus as she picked up the dying from the neglected streets of Calcutta. This saint and God were truly intimate friends.

However, my assumptions were challenged recently when National Public Radio produced a special on Mother Teresa after she was nominated to be canonized by the Roman Catholic Church. The reporter shared a captivating incident.

An unknown priest traveled to Calcutta to meet Mother Teresa. To his surprise he was given a private time with the aging nun. During the course of their conversation, he confessed, "Mother, I don't feel the presence of God in my life anymore."

"How long has it been?" she asked sensitively.

"About seven years," whispered the distraught priest. Mother Teresa pondered a moment, then reached out with compassion and touched the priest's hand.

"Seven years?"

"Yes, seven long years, Mother," replied the priest.

Mother Teresa paused, looked the priest in the eye, and whispered, "It has been over thirty for me."

This gentle woman with strong, penetrating eyes, who radiated joy, who boldly challenged world leaders, and who performed incredible acts of faith and charity, had not *felt* the presence of God in thirty years? I was stunned.

But the biography went on. In a letter to a friend, Mother Teresa penned, "I call, I cling, I want. The darkness is horrible." And to another, "The whole thing (God) might not be real." Interesting words from someone who had dedicated her entire life to serving God. Was there a disconnect? Was I missing something? Why would someone continue if he or she did not *feel* the presence of God in his or her life?

The report went on to say that Mother Teresa identified completely with Christ's sense of *abandonment*. Jesus confirmed this sense of abandonment when he suffered a cruel, unjustified death on the cross and cried out, "My God, my God, why have you forsaken me?" (Matt. 27:46). It was in Jesus that Mother Teresa found comfort—the Jesus who felt the pangs of isolation, separation, and abandonment.

I could more easily understand if those cries of despair came from the lips of a depressed philosopher who spent his life bemoaning his existential angst to a group of wide-eyed college sophomores. But hearing these words from a woman who faithfully started each morning with prayer and encouraged people to serve Jesus by caring for the poorest of the poor adds a new dimension to what it means to live a faith-filled life.

True faith, as personified in Mother Teresa, has nothing to do with scientific assurance, doctrinal boldness, or certitude. True faith is about how we choose to live our lives *despite* the doubts and feelings of separation from God. To be sure, her testimony is both liberating and frightening—liberating for those who desire to identify with Christian faith yet live each day crippled with questions and doubts; frightening because someone who appeared to be so close to God actually lived out her life feeling distant from God. One is forced to ask: Is this sense of alienation the reward for a life committed to faithful service? Is it like winning the booby prize for achieving first place?

Some might in despair conclude, "It is hypocritical for me to continue to espouse a belief in something that I don't really feel." And perhaps those people have a point. But Mother Teresa cuts against the grain of self-serving American Christianity. For she makes it clear that to truly identify with the Jesus of the cross, one must expect to feel some of the emotional isolation experienced on that cross. For Jesus, the cross was not just an instrument of physical brutality, was not only the excruciating pain of pierced hands and feet, it was the excruciating pain of wondering if that moment was the last of his moments. As a fully human man, bound by all the limitations of our humanity, Jesus felt totally *alone*. There was no cataclysmic intervening God to ease his pain. There was no mystical spirit to whisper words of comfort and solace. There were no feel-good optimists telling him that everything was going to be okay. None. Nothing. Only a solitary, broken man on a cross, wondering why the God of the universe had not rescued him from this calamity.

But abandonment and intense isolation are not feelings we like to identify with as Christians. Yes, we wear crosses around our necks and place them at the front of our sanctuaries, but few of us will embrace the full dimension of what it means to *take up your cross*. Mother Teresa took up the cross as she carried maggot-infested bodies and cried, "Where *are* you, God?" I am sure that as she struggled to stretch her limited budget to buy medicine and more beds, she wondered, "Where *are* you, God?" As she watched the hierarchies of her church argue over minutiae, she cried, "Where *are* you, God?" It would be difficult to live so close to so much misery and not wonder why God was so silent. It would take tremendous faith to continue.

Yet in and through her experiences, Mother Teresa encountered an aspect of Jesus few of us will ever know. And because of her identification with the abandoned Christ, she was able to persevere without the warm and assuring feelings so many of us long for. I find Mother Teresa's honesty compelling and am convinced that many other struggling souls would be relieved to find that they can believe in God, love God, serve God, and yet not continually *feel* God's presence. This is faith.

So many people associate faith with feeling a certain way about our relationship with God. If we "feel" close to God, we think our faith is strong. If we "feel" distant from God, we think our faith is weak. But what does Mother Teresa teach us about the relationship between faith and feelings? True faith—a faith that transcends feelings and emotional ups and downs—is expressed through committed acts of love. This is biblical faith. Mother Teresa teaches me that faith has little to do with my feelings. True faith is expressed through continued acts of selfless love. Sometimes I might feel God's presence. Other times I will not feel God's presence. Faith has nothing to do with my feeling.

Excuse Me, I Have an Opinion

Passive faith is a mark of self-satisfied, comfortable, well-educated people who can generally manipulate the variables of life toward their own end. . . . The faith I see in Abraham is proactive and risk-taking. It is to follow God into the un-

185

comfortable. It is setting out on an adventure, the dimensions of which we can't scope out ahead of time.

Gregory J. Ogden

"We definitely need a message from God: should we move forward by adding another grade to our school or not?"

The other board members nodded in agreement. They knew that over the past five years our Camden Forward School had added a new grade each year, with corresponding increases in our budget, teaching staff, and number of students. Happily, our small, alternative grade school had exceeded expectations—not only were our academic standards far above those of the public schools in the area but we had become God's hope for many families in our inner-city neighborhood as well. And because of generous donors, our tuition rates had been kept low, allowing the neediest of families to participate.

Was it time to take the next step? Should we add sixth, seventh, and eighth grades?

"What would be a *message from God?*" asked a board member.

I did a quick mental math calculation—salaries, benefits, curriculum materials, renovations, insurance, administrative additions for the next three years of expansion. "Say, $276,000," I replied, knowing the added figure was way beyond our abilities. I was convinced that we needed a major financial commitment to undergird the expansion so we would not have to struggle from year to year.

"Okay," said our board chairman, wanting to call the meeting to an end, "we'll make a decision at our next meeting. Bruce, you and the committee can make recommendations then. I move we adjourn."

It was two weeks before Christmas. I knew that January was a tough month for fund-raising, and certainly it was next to impossible to raise $276,000 in the next four weeks. We had no foundation proposals in the works. No

186

large donors were interested in this project—they didn't even know about it.

A few days later, in the midst of a busy morning, a middle-aged couple named George and Sophie Wright dropped by my office.

The couple turned out to have heard a little about our programs through a friend and wanted to see firsthand the work we were doing with children and teens. I had no idea why they were here. Some visitors come to offer advice on how to run things. Some come out of curiosity: "What in heaven's name goes on there?" Some volunteer generous amounts of time. Some give money. But who were the Wrights?

After leading a tour through our various programs and making spontaneous introductions to a few teachers and students, we ended up in my office for a time of . . . what? What was their interest? They had myriad questions about our school, its success rates, and its budgeting practices. I was caught up in the lively dialogue when there was a thump, thump, thump at the door.

I knew the sound. Surely it would be one of my staff standing in the doorway with a toilet plunger over his shoulder: "Got a minute? We have an emergency!"

But no, not this time. When I opened the door, there stood a four-foot two-inch, eleven-year-old student named Renaldo, not exactly my idea of the poster child who would impress a potential donor—a stained shirt, untied shoes, and ruffled hair.

"I have an opinion I need to share about the school," he blurted with no prelude, no explanation or polite greeting. He startled the Wrights. (I made a mental note to include manners in our curriculum—soon.)

"Uh . . . sure, Renaldo, sure," I stuttered, doubting whether I should have made the invitation.

"I just wanna say," he began, looking squarely at Mr. and Mrs. Wright with no clue who they were, "our school needs to add a sixth grade next year."

"Is that so you can continue at this fine school?"

"Nah." He was in his full stand-up comic mode. "It's not for me. I'll probably just be taking a break from school next year—you know, a little vacation."

"Thank you, Renaldo. Please return to class now." He turned and nonchalantly strolled down the hall, unaware that he had probably chilled some potential donors.

Sophie Wright turned to me. "What *is* going to happen next year?"

I explained that we were going to have to maintain the school at up to fifth grade and that kids like Renaldo would have to return to the public school system. And sadly, the system had an abysmal academic record.

"How much will it cost to add a new grade?" asked her husband.

"Well . . ."—I paused for a long moment—"about $276,000 for the next three years. I feel we really need a significant donor to make this commitment right up front so that we can build a quality program. Otherwise we'll be scrambling for funds, and our other grades will suffer."

"Thank you, Mr. Main, thank you. We'll be in touch."

Obviously they were touched by the children, impressed by the commitment of the teachers, and challenged by the potential of what had been and could be done. *Everyone is.* But it doesn't always mean that we'll hear from them again.

Two days later, however, Mrs. Wright called my office. She was eager to talk. I was surprised. "You wouldn't believe what happened today," she said excitedly. "I was wrapping up a deal today with a Geneva-based financial company—one of our brokerage firms—and we'd been working on this great project for the past three years. Our broker has become a good friend, and now it's time to phase out the account."

I began pacing around my desk. Where was all this going?

"Our broker, our friend," she chatted on, "asked me what I was going to do with my portion of the commission. Buy the silver Jaguar you've always wanted—the convertible one with chrome wheels?"

"The truth of the matter is that I *had* been talking with him about that silver Jaguar," said Mrs. Wright. "But after visiting your school, I began thinking. So I told him I was planning to send my commission to the school."

She paused.

"Our broker friend was speechless," she continued on. "He couldn't believe that I would just give my money away in that way. But he was intrigued, and he asked all sorts of impressive questions about your school. I sounded like your publicity director." She giggled again. "I told him that UrbanPromise was at a crossroads—trying to decide if you could add a new classroom and all that that implies. He asked me how much it would cost."

"So, what did you tell him?" I think I was holding my breath.

"Well, I just said $276,000. That's right, isn't it?"

"Yes," I agreed, trying to recalculate just to be sure. Where was this story going?

"Do you know what he said? He said that he'd cover that cost. All $276,000! Wasn't that nice? And he'll send you a letter of intent tomorrow. Now you can add the next three grades to your school!"

I sat down.

I regained my composure but was effusive with my thank-yous. I was deeply touched, and stunned, and in awe. And yes, after more thank-yous and good-byes, I hung up so that I could call my board of directors.

Most of the time when it's budget and payroll time, I grope along, hoping, praying, second-guessing, lying awake at night wondering if I have listened carefully and acted faithfully. But then I'm reminded of a favorite definition of faith, which comes from a professor at my seminary: Abraham, a man of faith, was the one who was called to go to *a place he knew not*. Faith is putting ourselves in situations where *if God doesn't show up, we're in trouble*.

As I reflect upon the life of Abraham, I am struck by how difficult and complex his life became *after* he responded in faith to the voice of God. Sure, there was the Promised Land. But there was also a famine and the confrontation with Egyptian leadership and lies about his wife. His cousin was kidnapped, and Abraham risked his life to rescue him. The crises seemed unending. Yet despite these difficulties, the promise is fulfilled.

Then there's Moses. He stood knee-deep in the Sea of Reeds as Pharaoh's army was closing in, about to slaughter everyone. Moses's leadership career was about to end. He was afraid, filled with doubt, wondering how he got himself into this situation. And then, *God showed up*.

It would be nice for me to relax now and revel in the joy of a big donation, a direct sign from God. But it will not be this way for long. Tomorrow, next week, next month I'll again find myself in a situation where if God doesn't show up, I'll be in deep trouble. Like a broken record, I will wonder, doubt, cry, pray, and whine.

And yet I am continually called to listen to God's voice and step out in faith—whether it is starting a new program, approaching someone who intimidates me and asking for money, releasing my need to control situations and instead trusting in the potential of those I have trained, or doing something that scares me to death. And yet, in each of these situations, when God shows up—however brief the moment—my faith is enriched and I get the opportunity to watch God work in some wonderfully mysterious ways.

Those who step outside the normal routines of their lives and place themselves in a position of reliance on God, Jesus consistently calls *people of faith*. The biblical story suggests that if we are to truly experience God in miraculous ways, we must place ourselves in a position where we are vulnerable and reliant on God. Waiting passively for God to show up and perform some kind of miracle does not seem to be the pattern. When was the last time you placed yourself in a situation where if God did not show up, you'd be in trouble? Is God calling you to take more risks in your life?

Terrorist of Love

> If change is to come, it will come from the margins. . . . It was the desert, not the temple, that gave us the prophets.
>
> Wendell Berry

It was one of those teachable moments—a special time when a class takes an unexpected turn, spontaneous dialogue erupts, internal lights of curiosity turn on, and real learning takes place. It's the kind of moment a teacher lives for.

My university class had just finished reading some fascinating and troubling material on the impact of sustained violence on children. Those sitting in our discussion circle had just read a research report about how children had suffered the horrible effects of the Khmer Rouge regime in Cambodia, the hideous evils of Renamo in Mozambique, and the despair of growing up in urban war zones in America. The researchers had written persuasively that those children who witness the brutal murder of a parent, an uncle, or a loved one will instinctively sense that the best revenge is violence. Children growing up in the midst of the Israeli–Palestinian struggle who had witnessed sustained violence were prime candidates for the creation of young terrorists. After all, they had become dehumanized and desensitized by their trauma—unable to empathize with those who held different beliefs or political positions.

"They didn't write about Northern Ireland," complained Roz in her thick Belfast brogue. She was a twenty-year-old sitting to my left. "There's three of us from Ireland in

191

this class," she continued. "We grew up with violence all around us. Although it was not as bad as that mentioned in the article, we *did* experience many of the same kinds of things."

The mood of the room shifted dramatically. The other students sat up straight and shook off their despondent gazes. Their academic assignment all of a sudden was no longer a disconnected book discussion. Their homework had become real.

"My father was killed by an IRA bomb when I was six," another young woman at the far end of the circle said abruptly. The class was silent, and I was caught off guard. Until this point in the semester, I had only really known the students by their quiz grades and their occasional comments in class. I had no idea that this reading material would hit so close to home.

"Aren't you angry, Cathy?" I asked her, wondering how a young woman whose father was brutally murdered could not be. "I mean, if anyone could be expected to be a terrorist, it should be you."

"No," she said without an edge to her voice. "I was raised in a home by a mother who taught me to forgive," she continued, "so the seeds of anger and bitterness never had a chance to grow. My mother modeled forgiveness for all us children."

I listened intently to this beautiful young woman. She had no hint of repressed bitterness in her voice. Rather, she had chosen to forgive, which obviously had made a profound difference for her. That choice had separated her from others her own age—others who had chosen to hold on to their anger, allowing it to fester into suppressed rage.

"I know lots of young people my age who are bitter, who are acting out violently. Some of them are even dead now. They just had to get in the last lick," said my young student.

"I'm adamantly against terrorism. Fighting terror with terror is not the way."

I could have ended the class at that point—probably even for the semester—because there wasn't much more to teach. She had said it all. And her life was a living testimony to the difference that a choice can make. *If each of the students could take this profound lesson from the classroom, I thought, and exercise its truth in their daily lives, the world would be a better place. A beautifully different place.*

I often wonder what the answer is for a world that continues to go to war and fight because of past wrongs. Will Israel and Palestine ever be able to live peacefully together? Will South Africa ever be able to move forward and overcome the horrible injustices of the past? Will places like Rwanda, Somalia, and Northern Ireland ever let go of the atrocities their citizens have committed against one another and create countries that are safe and just for all people? Can past wrongs based on racial inequalities ever be put to rest in our own country?

Not without forgiveness. Treaties can be signed, monetary compensations can be made, and political maneuvering can be orchestrated, but without forgiveness there will always be a need for revenge—without forgiveness those latent seeds of contempt will find expression.

How does one forgive? One can talk about forgiveness and argue for its importance on the basis of Scripture, but how do people forgive those who have hurt them, wronged them, abused them, or done evil against them or their loved ones? How do we move the idea of forgiveness from a theological belief to an action or decision that releases us from the bondage of hatred and anger?

To forgive another person takes a tremendous act of faith, because in forgiving we choose to surrender our need to control a situation to satisfy our longings and intentions. To transfer a situation or an event from our hands into God's takes a faith that goes beyond just lip service.

It may sound trite, but to make that kind of transfer requires one to believe that God has *witnessed the wrong* and that God *will not dismiss* that wrong as something trivial or insignificant. In the process of forgiving we say, "I give this situation to God and believe that in the eternal scheme of things, God's justice and grace will bring about a resolution better than I could ever make." To let go of our need to hit back, talk back, wall people out of our lives, retaliate, humiliate, malign, kill, or do whatever we desire allows us to trust God to bring about results in God's time. That then lifts us out of the realm of the temporal and places us in a realm governed by God. For most of us, no matter how serious we are about our faith, that kind of surrender is incredibly difficult. But it is possible. The results are glorious.

Fortunately, a mother in Northern Ireland fifteen years ago decided that her home would not become a haven of anger and hatred, a breeding ground for young terrorists. Instead, that mother chose to let God be God and not to take vengeance into her own hands. She placed herself in God's realm—she took the road of faith. Because of that choice, her twenty-year-old daughter now serves as a missionary to children in the inner city. She is a young woman who loves instead of hates, who gives life instead of destroying it, and who lives each day as a witness to the power of forgiveness.

It may seem a little odd to notice faith in a story that is basically about forgiveness. But in my experience, to truly forgive takes tremendous faith. It means giving up my need to control the outcome of a situation and trusting that the healthiest and most enduring resolution to a conflict is to act in the way prescribed by Jesus—and that means to forgive a person. Cathy embodied this kind of faith for me. Are there people you need to forgive as an act of faith? How can you be an agent of reconciliation in your community? In your family?

Lord,
How can I begin to live by faith?
How can I begin to live fully in the hope
that you can be trusted?
When those inclinations toward faith are birthed in
    me,
please grant the courage to listen
and respond with real steps and real acts—
not just for my benefit
but for the benefit of others in my midst.
Amen.

10

SACRIFICE NOTICED

Calling his disciples to him, Jesus said, "I tell you the truth, this poor widow has put more into the treasury than all the others."

Mark 12:43

The Gospel of Mark's account of the widow who put her few coins in the temple treasury implies that people regularly went to the temple to contribute. On the day of this unsettling account, a crowd of people was dropping money in the alms box—and Jesus was watching. In the midst of that seemingly ordinary event, Jesus *noticed* something a little unusual about to happen and alerted his disciples. The actions of an anonymous widow had caught his eye.

Mark's distinctive comment about her identity was that she was poor and a widow, the only two characteristics that define her as a person in the story. How did Jesus know that the woman was poor and a widow? Perhaps it was the way she dressed or that she was there alone in the temple—a woman shrouded in black without a male partner was often a cultural indicator—and being a widow in Jesus's day meant a life of poverty. Males provided the only economic support and protection for women. Jesus knew that. And those circumstances were what made her action so remarkable.

The writer Mary Anderson makes the point, commenting on this drama, that Jesus lifted the woman out of the *crowd*. By giving her last two coins in the temple, she had thrust herself into a position of total dependence on God. She had given *all* she had. And because of her willingness to surrender all, Jesus wanted the disciples to learn from her radical example. Jesus did not seem impressed with others' big or showy gifts. Nor was Jesus impressed with wealthy, powerful people. Jesus was impressed with what the gift represented.

What made the widow's gift so worthy of notice was the way it would impact her life: it would put her in a position of complete vulnerability. Mary Anderson applauds the woman's action by saying: "The issue is not how much we have in the bank, but what the money means for us. Is it our heart, our security, our source of power, or is it a tool for our stewardship? Are we dependent on our money to give us all we want and need from life, or are we dependent on God to make us rich?"[1] By giving all that she had as a gift to her God, the widow became a living example of sacrifice.

Both Jesus and Anderson emphasize that we must *notice* this woman's extravagant moment and allow her actions to penetrate our minds and hearts. Out of the crowd, out of the commonplace daily life of a person of no social stature, we discover a lesson to be learned about discipleship. The widow becomes "our spiritual mentor standing there on the margins of all we hold dear," continues Anderson. "Her way is a life of faith grounded in the love of God, the Holy Spirit. It's a life lived in the conviction that we are stewards of all we have in our hands and our lives, not the owners of these things."[2] So, compellingly, it was in the dank, labyrinthine halls of the temple one hot afternoon that Jesus taught his disciples a new lesson about stewardship, sacrifice, and faith.

Sadly, many of us would have missed the lesson altogether—even if we had been standing right next to Jesus. Why? Because most of us do not notice life as Jesus noticed life. I am sure I *would* have been impressed (and consequently blinded) by the large amounts of money being deposited by the wealthy temple-going contributors contemplating the new programs and new facilities that could be developed by such great gifts. Or perhaps I would have been numbed by the commonness and the daily routine of the moment. After all, it was just another day at the temple. Bells rang, merchants cajoled, sacrificial animals cooed and brayed and ran everywhere.

But as it turned out, it was not "just another day." In the midst of that ordinary day, Jesus was about to immortalize an anonymous widow and make her for centuries the subject of uncounted sermons, commentaries, and theological discussions. Her life continues to speak to us today.

Jesus identified this woman and, by extension, other ordinary, faithful people as living illustrations of a faithful life. Through her Jesus made graphic his teachings on stewardship, sacrifice, and faith, which were too abstract for some. The master teacher, always creative, often so pointed, found another way to illustrate his words with a real-life example. Sure, Jesus used words to teach his disciples about loving God and loving their neighbor. But consistently we see him making a point of finding ordinary people who put his teachings into practice, then using those people to illustrate his truths. Jesus knew the difference between words and the implementation of words. In the widow, Jesus found a real-life model of someone who authentically lived in proper relationship to material possessions.

CONTEMPLATING SACRIFICE

The story of the widow is particularly meaningful to me; it haunts me, is etched in my conscience, and tries to keep me centered on what God truly values.

As part of my job, I must raise thousands of dollars each month to pay the bills to keep the inner-city ministry I direct solvent. Each week I receive gifts from supporters who send five dollars and supporters who send thousands of dollars. An obvious temptation for me is to favor those who send the big gifts—to send special notes, to make appreciative phone calls, or to invite them to special VIP events. It is a temptation that all Christian leaders struggle to resist. But the unnamed widow of this story reaches across my desk and reminds me that those who give big gifts actually may not be giving much in God's economy. She reminds me that those who are giving the smaller gifts may actually be giving "bigger" gifts in God's eyes. The widow provides a new gauge for measuring generosity.

But just as the widow continues to guide me, so do the testimonies and lives of other people who give sacrificially. Those people challenge me to reevaluate my own willingness to give; they challenge my resistance to part with my money, time, and resources. They also speak to me as does the widow.

I need to see living illustrations of sacrifice in the ordinary places of my life. But things get in the way. Sometimes it is my busy schedule. Other times it is the pervasive examples of greed and self-preservation that subtly and seductively block my line of vision. Contemporary media feed me a distorted diet of materialism's promises: *Borrow, borrow, borrow so I can accumulate more, more, more—satisfaction promised! Live beyond my means, even if it means accruing debt—the newest and shiniest will bring happiness!* My family and I are impacted by the message and all too easily become intoxicated by these illusions of self-sufficiency and power. With the messages continually infiltrating our eyes, our ears, our hearts, and our minds, it becomes difficult to notice those who counter our culture and model the heart of God. I need to notice these alternative models of faith and stewardship—sadly, in our day, they are sometimes hard to find.

So let's engage our imaginative thinking, sparked by the widow in the temple in Jerusalem, and sit just to the right and a little behind Jesus—and watch. Let's learn to watch in our jobs. In our neighborhoods. In our churches. Or maybe we need to get out of our neighborhoods and go watch in those places where people live closer to the edge. And if we find those who hold the treasures of this world lightly, will we allow ourselves to be convicted by their testimonies? Will we allow the prophetic nature of their actions to penetrate our hearts and challenge us to do likewise? If we do, we will begin down the path of greatness—greatness as Jesus defined the term.

STORIES OF SACRIFICE NOTICED

Sacrifice has become a bad word in our culture. Everything around us tells us to look out for ourselves and get all that we can. Each day our consumer culture sends thousands of messages reminding us that we deserve more and need more. We are told that our lives are incomplete and empty if we do not buy their products. Yet underneath the assault of messages and images, we know that it is all a lie. More "stuff" will never satisfy our deepest longings. The accumulation of the "new and improved" will only give our lives temporary meaning. Jesus reminds us that to find life, we must be willing to give up our lives. It is in this "dying to self" that we begin to experience a life of greater abundance and greater joy. Ordinary people who understand this truth become living examples of how this principle plays out in daily life.

The Unlikely Giver

As a preacher, as a teacher, you are more important than
anything you say. You are the curriculum. In a real sense,
you are the sermon.

David Hubbard

As I was washing the dishes one Sunday afternoon, the
TV happened to be on. I caught the tail end of an interesting
documentary on PBS. It was honoring the recipients of the
Jefferson Award—an award given to ordinary citizens who
do extraordinary things. One of the recipients caught my
attention. His name was Art Dawson.

For the past forty years, the announcer said, Art Dawson had worked for the Ford Motor Company as a forklift
operator—working six, sometimes seven days a week and
usually putting in twelve-hour shifts. He had a one-bedroom
apartment and a very simple lifestyle. He appeared to be a
very humble, hardworking, blue-collar kind of guy. Surprisingly, Dawson was being honored as a philanthropist!

Now, when I hear the word *philanthropist*, I don't usually
think of a person who fits Art's profile. Philanthropists are
venture capitalist–types, men and women who start high-
tech businesses and sell them for gazillions of dollars—and
already have stock portfolios as thick as telephone books.
Or now more frequently they are highly paid athletes or
actors lending their names to charities as they make their
highly publicized gifts.

No, they are not forklift operators with seventh-grade
educations, nor were they raised in abject poverty. They are
not the Art Dawsons of the world.

The announcer went on to say with appropriate excitement in his voice that over the past ten years Art Dawson had
given $1.5 million in scholarship money to young university
students who came from impoverished backgrounds. Every
extra penny Dawson had earned throughout his career had

been saved in an effort to give to others. His choice to live simply and invest his money in blue chip stocks, combined with his fierce determination to help others, had made this humble man a significant philanthropist. He had helped hundreds of students who never thought they had a dream of making it into college get the kind of education he never had. When asked what had motivated his generosity, he simply said that he wanted to see young people get what he never had the opportunity to receive—a university degree.

For me, the highlight of the program was listening to the students who had benefited from Dawson's incredible generosity. Student after student shared how a few extra dollars for books or tuition made the difference. Furthermore, the students were awed by the source of their scholarships and amazed to discover who their unusual benefactor was. It gave them increased inspiration and dedication to their studies.

After watching that ten-minute segment about Art Dawson, I reflected on what God can do through those who love to give—the kind of giving that is not based on what is left over when all our spending is done. Art lived life in reverse: he lived and worked so he could give to others.

The postmodern generation often applauds itself on moving beyond rigid commitments and stifling rituals, yet the concept of giving *as a first priority* is the biblical model. It seems apparent from both the Old and New Testaments that God wants us to develop hearts and minds that think of giving *first*. Art Dawson embodied that attitude—he lived to give.

As the director of an organization that exists because of the benevolence of others, I have learned something about people who give. Giving has nothing to do with how much a person possesses or earns. People who give do so regardless of how much they own, how much they make, or how secure their financial situations might be. Giving is an attitude. It is a lifestyle. Giving is a matter of the heart. It is a discipline.

Over the years I have met multimillionaires who struggle to part with one dime. But happily I have met welfare moms who turn their heat to fifty degrees during the winter and forgo meat in favor of macaroni and cheese just so they can joyously make an offering to God's work each week. And many times notes from donors are attached to the gifts sent to our mission organization. The notes are remarkable and tell of heroic generosity. "My husband was just laid off from his job, but we want you to have this little bit of money for the children. I know it is not much, but I hope it helps." Or from the widow on a fixed income, "My heating oil was cheaper this winter, so here is what I was able to save." These short notes are incredibly humbling and remind me that many people give faithfully and sacrificially and are never noticed.

Of course, many wealthy people also give anonymously and humbly as they choose to live out their faith with little fanfare. They desire no building to be built in their honor, no press release to be sent to the local newspapers, and no VIP treatment when visiting our programs. The dollar amounts of their checks are significant, yet no one ever knows of their gifts. They walk away from the seductive temptations their gifts offer them—a heightened sense of importance and self-worth. In so doing they have internalized the biblical mandate that when one gives to the needy, "do not announce it with trumpets" (Matt. 6:2).

Paul's words to the church of Corinth established a wonderful giving principle:

> Remember this—a farmer who plants only a few seeds will get a small crop. But the one who plants generously will get a generous crop. You must each make up your own mind as to how much you should give. Don't give reluctantly or in response to pressure. For God loves the person who gives cheerfully.
>
> 2 Corinthians 9:6–7 NLT

Something wonderful happens when we plant generously. In the act of giving beyond what is practical and prudent, our hearts are enlarged, our priorities are altered. And thus we learn to loosen our grip on the enticing, ephemeral things of this world and instead embrace the generous, sacrificial things that are eternal—opening our lives to the potential of reaping generously.

This year let us be like Art Dawson, the forklift operator from Michigan who made $17 an hour, who has single-handedly enabled a small army of impoverished kids to become doctors, scientists, social workers, teachers, and pastors, all of whom are making a difference in their communities.

Do you *live to give*? I wonder what the world would look like if we all adopted this motto for our lives. Art Dawson's remarkable testimony reminds me that meaning, life purpose, and joy do not come from looking out for myself. They come from investing in things that have eternal value—things that last beyond the life of a new car, piece of clothing, or Rolex watch. Art Dawson challenges me to reevaluate my priorities. Not that he makes me feel guilty about wanting stuff. But he reminds me of the opportunity I possess to bless others.

Finished by One

It's never too late to be what you might have been.

George Eliot

After thirty years of teaching high school literature, Ms. Rogers was happy to retire. The years of lesson plans, delinquent students, and weekends spent grading papers were over—it was time to enjoy life. Perhaps she'd find an hour or two to volunteer at her church. Maybe a few hours at a local charity wouldn't hurt. Nothing strenuous. Probably just a morning a week. Well, maybe two—max—but only *after* a long, exotic vacation.

So one morning after her two months of retired living, Ms. Lynne Rogers was ready to volunteer her services—just one morning a week—just to help a few teenagers struggling with their writing. She asked me, "Does your ministry need anyone who has taught young people?"

What Ms. Rogers could not have realized was that the principal of our small high school had felt a change of life direction and resigned the previous day. With no captain steering, our school was in for a rough semester. School was to start in two weeks. Where was I going to find a qualified person to take charge at this late date?

Twenty minutes into giving a tour through our facilities while talking glowingly about our exceptionally diverse programs, I offered Ms. Rogers the job of principal. Although she had no administrative experience, I thought her teaching record was enough to warrant a try. She was not quite as eager! The blank stare with which she responded to my offer indicated that an administrative post was the least of her ambitions at this retired stage of her life. She was not going to bite my baited hook. "I'm not really qualified," she assured me. "I just want an hour or two as a volunteer. I'm sure you'll find someone," she said firmly.

I shifted to my begging mode. "Ms. Rogers, the future of the school will be jeopardized without an experienced leader. Struggling teens will never be transformed—there will be no college for them." I promised that this selfless commitment would be an amazing legacy for her—a decision that would create a whole new generation of leaders for our community.

There was silence. I didn't say a word.

"If . . . just if . . . now, don't hurry me . . . if I should even *consider* taking the job, I'd have to finish by one o'clock each day," Ms. Rogers said. "I've other commitments, you know."

I concealed my excitement. The door was open—a crack.

"I can work with that," I said gently so that I wouldn't scare her off. "I mean, all you will need to do is be present to start the school day and then make sure the afternoon classes are scheduled with other teachers." I was ready to make any kind of concession. Ask anything; I will agree. Fresh coffee ready in the teachers' lounge by 7:00 a.m.? *No problem.* A reserved parking space? *Absolutely.* Extra personal days? *We'll negotiate.* All I knew was that I did not want to be running a school in two weeks—I was overwhelmed already.

Lynne Rogers took the job.

Her first year was incredible. The retired teacher turned administrator approached her new vocation with extraordinary enthusiasm and vigor. She loved being in an environment where she could integrate her faith with her teaching. "I've been waiting my entire career for this opportunity. It never could have happened in a public school," she told me. The staff were happy with her leadership. Students were learning at accelerated rates. Lynne Rogers was *having the time of her life.*

What intrigued me most about this reluctant lady was the hours she worked. In the morning her car was always in the parking lot before mine. At four, often five o'clock—well after the other teachers had gone home for the day—guess what? Lynne Rogers was still at work.

"It's a little past 1:00 p.m.," I would chide her as she walked to her car, while I grinned and pointed at my watch—the little hand on the five, the big hand on the twelve. Of course, she remembered our conversation at the negotiation table and chuckled. That whole first year she *never* left the school at 1:00.

One Saturday I went to the office to catch up on some work, as I often did. To my surprise, Lynne's car was parked in her favorite spot. Saturday morning at 9:00 a.m.! I could not resist the opportunity to tease her one more time.

"Lynne!" She looked up, startled. "Are you going to get home before 1:00?" We both laughed as she pushed aside the stack of half-graded papers.

"You know," she said, "when I'm involved in something that seems to be making a difference—that's really changing lives—I don't think about the time."

As I have watched Lynne Rogers at work, I have seen someone who has found her calling. She has joy as she works with her students, an enthusiasm that exudes to the staff, and a commitment that forgets about the clock. Ms. Rogers has found a faith community where she can use the gifts and talents God has allowed her to develop over the years. And now God's transforming power is being released in magnificent ways to those who come into her path.

Surveys I read about employment satisfaction indicate that most workers dislike their jobs. Numerous millions count the hours until closing each day. Consequently, their spirits lose their luster and sense of meaning. Tragically, these workers fail to maximize their God-given potential.

Lynne Rogers reminds me that if we are willing to step out in faith and sacrifice our time and resources, we may find that place where it really does not matter if we finish by 1:00.

How closely do you guard your time? How closely do you guard your resources? The great tragedy of so many lives is that people get up each morning and spend the bulk of their time doing something they do not enjoy. Why? Let's be honest: most of the time it is because we need the money. But is life not more than just making a living? Our lives are so short. Why spend them doing something that does not use our gifts and bring us joy? Oddly, joy and contentment are often found in doing those things that the world would deem a "sacrifice"—working at a job that gives us fulfillment rather than a good paycheck, volunteering in our free time, and giving of our resources to help other people. Lynne's life can challenge us to re-evaluate our current situation and consider thinking about a life change.

The Eternal Implications of Small Acts

By whatever we do, we either advance or obstruct the drama of redemption; we either reduce or enhance the power of evil.

Abraham Heschel

"If it weren't for that day outside my school when Judy put a flyer in my hand, I don't know where I'd be today." She paused for a long moment. "I sure wouldn't be here. I'd never even have heard of Howard University. I would have never gone to college."

Rosy was calling me from an office building in Chicago. I remembered this vivacious young woman as first an awkward seventh grader, then a teenager who struggled with depression and low self-esteem. I remembered that her father had succumbed to drug addiction. Her mother had lost the struggle to keep the family together, and her younger sister had become pregnant with a second child.

In the midst of all of her family turmoil, Rosy never believed she was smart enough to attend college. No one in her family had ever gone beyond high school. Why would it be any different for her?

But now as a college junior she had been selected from an elite group of college students to do a summer internship with Allstate Insurance Company.

"I don't believe it," she said, practically bubbling over. "They *flew* me out here! They picked me up in a stretch limo from O'Hare. I'm staying in a condo that has a Jacuzzi, a huge swimming pool, and *maid service*! Bruce, they even do my laundry! Can you believe it? I get fresh towels every day. It's surreal."

"Hooray for you, Rosy!" I said, remembering that only a few months earlier she had been discouraged and ready to drop out of college. She could not afford to make her tuition payments.

"You won't believe this, Bruce, but last weekend they took us horseback riding. I'd never been on a horse before, and, sure, I still ache—but it was *fantastic.*"

As we hung up, one statement just hung in the air: "If it weren't for that day outside my school when Judy put a flyer in my hand, *I don't know where I'd be today.*"

Because of the faithfulness of a practically forgotten volunteer, Rosy's life had taken a dramatic turn. Instead of taking a nap one afternoon, instead of watching a soap opera, going to the mall, or reading a book, one of our volunteers went the extra mile. Because of her extra commitment—her selfless initiative—the whole course of Rosy's life had been altered. Judy's flyer that ended up in Rosy's hand turned Rosy on to our ministry. That moment changed her life by beginning a whole series of positive choices, positive experiences, and encounters with positive people.

How much do our actions matter? Did a decision between taking a nap or passing out flyers really make the difference in lifting a young woman out of a life of struggle and poverty? Would Rosy's life be completely different today if she had not received that little slip of paper?

Sometimes Christians have a tendency to emphasize God's will and minimize the effects of human will. Over the years I have often heard volunteers say after a few days of service, always with tears in their eyes, "I need to move on—but I'll pray that God sends someone to take care of these kids." They fail to see the connection between their commitments, their actions, their decisions, and the potential impact they have on the lives of the kids they had come to serve. For some reason they believe that *God* will magically take care of things.

The reality is, God does not take care of those kids whom *we* are called to take care of. Rather, those kids' lives are profoundly impacted by the *absence* of a caring adult. They are not magically mentored; they are not nurtured by some computer they sit in front of between 3:00 and 6:00 p.m.

Those kids we think, or hope, God is supposed to take care of end up getting abused, dropping out of school, selling drugs, or getting pregnant because they have no caring, committed person in their lives.

The movie *Schindler's List* is a powerful portrayal of the significance of one human life. Oskar Schindler, through his creative willingness to risk his own life to save others, managed to save thousands of Jews from extermination in the Second World War. Schindler was a businessman who used his position to employ Jews. Instead of turning a blind eye to the problems that resulted from a distorted nationalism and racial bigotry, like so many of his contemporaries did, Schindler risked his life for others. He did not believe that somehow *God* would save the Jewish people from the gas chambers.

At the end of the film was a stunningly dramatic moment. The Germans had lost the war. Jews were being released from those devastatingly evil prison camps around Eastern Europe. Schindler was at his factory, surrounded by throngs of barely surviving Jews who were thanking him for saving their lives because of his courage to create illegal jobs. At this moment that should have been a celebration, Schindler realized that he could have done more—*he could have saved more lives.* The weight of that responsibility settled upon him. He began to cry. He stripped off his ring and said with enormous anguish, "If only I had sold it, I could have saved another ten people." He looked at the other material things that he had held on to and realized that the money could have been used to save other people. The weight of his responsibility was overwhelming.

Austin Farrer, a British theologian, argued persuasively that God works in the world when divine intentions are coupled with human intentions. He called it a theology of the *double will.* In effect, he argued that when the divine will and the human will combine, God's presence can truly

211

be released to move in the world. His strong point is that *both wills are needed.*

This theology of the double will was played out one lazy summer afternoon when one of my volunteers decided to forgo her afternoon nap and instead pass out promotional flyers for our summer camp—to just a bunch of ragtag, unsuspecting seventh graders. Her decision, an eternal decision, made all the difference in the world—to at least one person.

How much do our actions matter? What is the relationship between God's ability to act in the world and our laziness? How much do we limit God's actions because of our decisions and our perception that our choices do not matter? These are questions we must ponder as we consider the notion of sacrificially giving our time and attention to others. I believe we underestimate the tremendous impact our lives and actions can have in shaping the future of our world. When we give to others of our time and attention, the potential to ignite God's movement in the world is tremendous.

Six Professors

What marks us in the eyes of our enemies is our practice of loving-kindness: "Only look," they say, "look how they love one another!"

Tertullian, *Apology*

The staff sat around five folding tables for our annual half-day retreat. Many of them were new, nervous, and eager to get a sense of their surroundings. The facilitator gave her standard warm-up routine and a joke that didn't do very well, cleared her throat, then started with, "Who can share a situation wherein God provided for one of your specific material needs?" Surprisingly, hands popped up.

"I needed some money to buy a plane ticket so that I could come here and be a part of the team. Sure enough, two days before I needed to purchase the ticket, the money arrived from an unexpected source," claimed twenty-year-old Greer. Everyone in the group applauded. I even heard a "Praise the Lord" from the back table.

"I've raised five children, seven grandchildren, and eight great-grandchildren," volunteered one of the older members of the group. "There was a time when I was out of money and had no idea how I was going to feed my five kids. I got down on my knees, prayed to God, and would you believe it? Groceries arrived every day that week. I didn't ask anyone. *They just arrived.*" The group broke into wild applause.

To my right stood a young woman named Fran. She was new to our staff, and her voice hinted at her nervousness. "At college I was getting notices in my mailbox every week—you know, those notices that say, 'If you don't pay your bill by 3:00 p.m. Friday, you'll be asked to leave school.'" We all nodded as we recalled our own college days—days of working part-time to cover tuition and books. "My parents had just divorced," she said, trying to keep control, "and there was no money available for me. Well, I just packed my car with all my stuff and was driving toward the campus gates." She paused. "On an impulse I decided to stop and say good-bye to one of my favorite professors. I walked into his office and said, 'I have to leave school.'

"He was really shocked. And I'll never forget his words: 'What do you mean, you're leaving school? Why, you're one of our best students. You can't quit, you *have* to finish.'

"'I just don't have the money,' I told him, looking at the floor. 'I've got a big balance on my bill.'

"He said with growing exasperation, 'Have you gone to the accounting office and checked?'

"'No . . . not in the last few days,' I confessed.

"'Well, before you leave, just do me a favor—go check it out.'

"Puzzled and annoyed, I went to the accounting office and asked, 'Could you please tell me what my tuition balance is? *Zero?* How's that possible?' The woman behind the desk simply replied that an anonymous person had paid it." Fran was now a little more choked up, but she continued. "For the next year and a half, every time I got my bill, there was a notation on it that said, 'Your balance had been paid by an anonymous donor.'"

We were all intrigued—and even if she had stopped her story then, I would have been impressed. Obviously God had provided for her, and she completed college with honors.

"But," she continued, "it was at graduation, when I walked across the platform with all the other graduates to receive my diploma, that the president of the college also slipped me a small envelope. Well, I sure was startled—and curious—since no one else had received one. When I got back to my seat I opened the note. Do you know what it said?"

Well, tell us, tell us, I wanted to shout!

"There was a big, beautiful, embossed word on the card: 'Congratulations!' It was signed by my six professors. *They were the anonymous givers!* They had paid my college bill for my last year and a half."

Most people can guess how much professors earn at small Christian colleges: not much. But in spite of that, those professors gave generously enough to get a young woman through college—a young woman who otherwise might never have graduated. Indeed, their sacrificial giving left an indelible impact on Fran, who will never forget their acts of love. Those acts still guide her decisions and impact her actions. Her professors' surprising and sacrificial gift now fuels *her* passionate gift for service. The six professors certainly continue to give lectures to thousands of students and because of their wisdom have published prestigious articles in scholarly journals. And just as certainly, most of their words have been forgotten. But their gifts have not been forgotten. They transcended the rhetoric and continue to speak to and guide a wonderful young woman who is making a difference in our world.

What is the purpose of sacrificial giving? Is it to fulfill some kind of obligation? Is it to gain spiritual brownie points with God? I don't think so. The opportunity to sacrifice is a gift—an opportunity to bless others, to encourage others, and to reflect the heart of God in our world. Is there someone in your world whose life could potentially be transformed by your gift of time, attention, or resources? Six professors have changed the course of history. The young woman they touched will touch others, and in turn those people will touch others. The six professors have initiated a redemptive circle that will continue long beyond their lives.

> Lord,
> We like to think we are in control of our lives.
> We struggle with letting go of "our" stuff.
> We think money and possessions buy life,
> buy contentment, and buy our security.
> Yet we know deep inside that abundant life,
> true contentment, and true security are found only in
>   you.
> Help us to see those who understand what it means
>   to truly give,
> and help us to respond to the challenge of their lives.
> Help us to remember that abundant life is found in
>   giving away our lives.
> Amen.

11

THE UNNOTICED NOTICED

"What do you want me to do for you?" Jesus asked him.

Mark 10:51

I had just finished preaching. An elderly woman approached me in the receiving line. Her accent was thick, suggesting a recent arrival in the States. Strangely, I thought, she wanted me to know that her assimilation to Western life had been difficult. She found the absence of community in North America to be a tremendous void in our culture. "We may have war in Iraq," she said with her heavy accent, "but we do not have loneliness. You see, in my country, nobody drinks coffee alone."

Nobody drinks coffee alone! What a critique of our culture. For this perceptive woman, the threat of war had been tolerable and living under the continued oppression of a dictator had been manageable. But what she found truly difficult was making a smooth transition to our culture of individualism, lack of community, and little personal contact. Perhaps we have a Starbucks on every corner, we enjoy our four freedoms, we live in peaceful neighborhoods, and we don't worry about suicide bombers on our buses every morning during our daily commute. But despite our obvious blessings, many people, like my new friend, are lonely, forgotten, and living in isolation. Thousands of people in our cities are alienated from positive relationships with family, neighbors, civic groups, and churches. Just as Bartimaeus, the blind beggar in Mark's Gospel, sat at the side of the road, people on the fringes of our culture cry, "Somebody, please, somebody . . . have mercy on me."

The late Mother Teresa of Calcutta made a similar comment during a visit to the United States. Mother Teresa—that wonderfully dedicated nun living under a vow of poverty, who continually and without fanfare picked up the dead and dying from the streets of Calcutta—spent a few weeks visiting various ministries throughout the eastern United States. It was her first visit to America, and her reputation as a religious icon was growing, so a number of reporters followed her from place to place. One of them, looking for an impressive quote, asked how the poverty of the United States compared with the poverty of Calcutta. To the reporter's surprise, Mother Teresa said, "Oh, the poverty in the United States is *much greater* than the poverty of Calcutta."

The reporter was perplexed. "What do you mean? How can the poverty in the United States possibly compare to that of Calcutta?"

Mother Teresa, never afraid to give a direct and candid answer, looked at the brash reporter with her sparkling eyes and said simply, "The poverty in Calcutta is physical, but in the United States the poverty is the disease of loneliness. *It is the poverty of being nobody to anybody.*"

Nobody to anybody! According to Mother Teresa, poverty is deeper than just a lack of physical resources—not having enough food, living in a cardboard box, not having medical care. She felt that eating meager portions of food and living in inadequate conditions does not always mean having no joy, no friends, or no community. *Being poor* concerns a person's whole being—physical, spiritual, emotional, and sense of well-being.

Not surprisingly, in the Gospels we discover a Jesus who was genuinely and frequently concerned with people who were poor in spirit and in health and who were alienated from enriching relationships in a social and religious community. But Jesus noticed them. He drew them out of the shadows and welcomed them onto the path of restoration. And restoration always begins with *noticing*. Only after *noticing the unnoticed* can something be done to change the circumstances of the poor.

NOTICING "NOBODIES"

Our Gospel stories are full of examples of Jesus noticing those whom others overlooked—people who were *nobody to anybody*. Whether it was a blind beggar by the side of the road, a group of lepers stigmatized as untouchable, or a forgotten woman living under the veil of shame due to chronic bleeding, Jesus noticed those whom others blindly walked past or dismissed.

But let's go back to Bartimaeus (see Mark 10:46–52). He is one of the best examples of noticing, as Jesus encountered him blind, begging, and sitting on the road outside the city of Jericho, dependent on the charity of indifferent strangers. Few things could be worse than waking up each morning to sit again on a pile of Mediterranean rocks for ten hours of sightless isolation. I am sure that few stopped to talk. No, just the distant chatter of people passing by—businessmen contriving a deal, young couples whispering affections, children laughing, and rabbis verbally dissecting their laws. Sure, people threw a coin to him once in a while, but did they ever stop to talk, to touch, to ask a question, or to treat him like a fully human being? Not likely. So Bartimaeus sat there year after year, lonely and invisible.

But Jesus modeled for us all the true act of *noticing*. Above the buzz of the crowds, Jesus heard the cry of Bartimaeus and stopped. "Call him," he said (v. 49). Jesus invited the beggar to come out of the shadows of obscurity. The indifferent, often hostile crowd wanted to keep the beggar invisible, in the background, but Jesus brought him into the full view of everyone. Then Jesus did something truly radical (as he so often did): he asked Bartimaeus a question! Jesus did not impose himself, his remedies, or his agenda on Bartimaeus, for Bartimaeus had already experienced a lifetime of snarling judgments: "If your mother hadn't been such a sinner, maybe you wouldn't have ended up this way." "If you'd spent more time in prayer, God would have healed you."

Rather, Jesus asked in nearly a whisper, "What do you want me to do for you?" (v. 51). He shocked his audience.

Yet in simply asking Bartimaeus that question, Jesus modeled the true *act of noticing*. For noticing involves more than just a glance, a fleeting comment, a passing smile, or a few coins in a hat. Noticing engages and affirms a person. And Jesus engaged a beggar who was nobody to anybody. By asking Bartimaeus a question, Jesus empowered him to suggest his own prescription. That was not charity, for charity seldom considers the feelings or humanity of the receiver; it just assumes that *they* need something and that *our* help is what they need. But because Jesus affirmed Bartimaeus's full worth as a human being, Bartimaeus responded enthusiastically, "Oh, Rabbi, yes, yes, I want to see!" (see v. 51).

I find Jesus's act of noticing extremely challenging when I remember how close Jesus was to death. A few verses earlier (33–34) Jesus announces that his time on earth is drawing to a close. If the present journey is continued, Jesus understands that he will end up in the hands of those who will kill him. For many of us, the certainty of a cruel death would create a heightened sense of distraction, anxiety, and urgency—potentially shifting our priorities, focus, and ideals. Not for Jesus. Jesus's commitment to noticing the unnoticed remains central to his mission despite the conflict awaiting him in Jerusalem.

The most significant person ever to walk the earth, under the pressure of imminent death, noticed and stopped for somebody who was nobody to anybody! Bartimaeus could do nothing for Jesus. He could not protect him from death. He could not advance Jesus's career or his reputation. Jesus faced the chance that Bartimaeus might not even appreciate his help and precious time. But Jesus, though surely immersed in the anxiety of his own impending death, remained true to what it meant to live a noticing life.

If I knew I were in my last days on earth, my temptation would be to maximize those final hours by spending time with important people or people who loved me—people who might continue my legacy in some capacity. If you are like me, you might pack your Palm Pilot or Day-Timer with appointments, schedule some time in isolation with family and those you love, or try to write down your final words of wisdom. Our eyes would be riveted on the next important event, the next appointment, or getting our personal items in order.

THE CONSEQUENCES OF NOT NOTICING

Jesus not only models this idea of noticing people who are often overlooked and invisible but also underscores the importance of this practice for each of us. One of the most powerful examples of this idea is found in the story Jesus told of a rich man and a beggar named Lazarus. Luke 16:19–31 recounts for us the story of the rich man who enjoyed all the benefits of "the good life"—beautiful clothing, a house with a gate, an abundance of food. In contrast, the poor man, Lazarus, sat and slept just outside the rich man's gate; he was covered with sores and longed to eat just the crumbs from the rich man's table.

The only virtue of Lazarus (whose name ironically means "he whom God helps") seemed to be that he lived at the rich man's gate. Interestingly, Jesus made no reference to Lazarus's upstanding piety or the good works he had committed—there were none. Lazarus was known only for his poverty. And Jesus heightens for his listeners the sense of poverty's grinding inequities by noting that Lazarus lived against the backdrop of the rich man's life, on the doorstep of the rich man. Accordingly, as the rich man returned home each day, he would pass that dreadful wretch Lazarus. The wealthy man walked past the annoying sight of the man covered in sores, crying out for food. He paid no notice. He did not allow Lazarus's condition to impact his heart. Familiarity, even with poverty and destitution, can lead to contempt.

But then Jesus's story takes a strange twist: the poor man ended up with a favored eternal position. Oh, the radical inclusion of God! That came as a shock to Jesus's listeners. That's why New Testament theologian Charles H. Talbert suggests that "a parable that portrayed its hero as an unclean beggar must have been as startling to Pharisaic assumptions (in their eyes the concept of being ceremonially clean—Lazarus was considered ceremonially unclean because dogs licked his sores—plus rich equaled a righteous man) as one that depicted a Samaritan as hero."[1] Lazarus as hero of the story would be an affront to all those who heard.

And in an even greater twist, the rich man consequently ends up in hell. Jesus's story suggests that the basis of the rich man's eternal damnation had nothing to do with shaky synagogue attendance, infidelity, or personal integrity. But his personal damnation was connected to his inability to truly notice someone in need and respond in a way that shared his resources.

Dr. Martin Luther King Jr., commenting on Jesus's story, made an insightful point in a sermon he preached during the civil rights era. King pointed out that it was not the man's wealth that cast him into eternal hell. After all, King noted, Abraham was one of the wealthiest men spoken of in the Old Testament, yet he had favored status in heaven. No, what King suggested was that the rich man chose not to *notice* the poor man at the gate. Wealth was not the problem—although Jesus does warn us in other teachings of its dangers. The problem was that the rich man did not notice and respond to Lazarus's hunger and physical needs. According to Jesus, indifference, or not noticing, was why the rich man ended up in hell.

Furthermore, it was no accident that Luke placed this parable just a few verses after Jesus's scathing rebuke of the Pharisees and their love for money. Jesus summed up his rebuke by claiming, "What is prized by human beings is an abomination in the sight of God" (Luke 16:15 NRSV). Thus the parable of Lazarus becomes a reminder to us that if we spend our lives trying to impress our neighbors, our colleagues, and the people who sit next to us on Sunday mornings, then we are failing to notice what really counts. What really counts is whether we see the overlooked and forgotten in our midst. In Jesus's estimation, not noticing the poor has dire spiritual consequences.

CONTEMPLATING THE UNNOTICED

I know a young man named Shane Claiborne. After graduating from college, he encouraged some friends to move with him into a run-down row house in North Philadelphia. Shane was convinced that the best way to notice the poor was to build relationships with them, and the best way to build relationships was to live among them. In a recent interview Shane commented:

> I recently surveyed people who said they were "strong followers of Jesus." Over 80 percent agreed with the statement, "Jesus spent much time with the poor." Yet only 1 percent said that they themselves spent time with the poor. We believe we are following the God of the poor—yet we never truly encounter the poor.[2]

What Shane simply illustrates is that interactions between people of different socioeconomic groups seldom occur within the Christian community. Intellectually we may assent to the belief that God is among the poor and calls his followers to be with the poor, but existentially this truth is not acted upon. If we want to notice the poor, we need to put ourselves in situations where we can meet them.

Each summer the ministry I direct brings hundreds of college-age students to the inner city. The students come from middle- and upper-middle-class homes around the world to spend a summer living in the poorest urban neighborhoods in America. During the course of the summer, these students—many of whom have never met a poor person—eat dinner with their neighbors, play checkers or baseball with poor families, and have other interactions to purposely develop relationships. It is within the context of building relationships that their eyes are opened and they begin to see life through the eyes of those who have little. Often the experience is life-changing. One student named Lynne recently wrote me:

> I came back heartbroken from the sights I had seen and the lives that had touched my own. My eyes were very much opened to areas I had never seen before . . . so thanks for helping me to see Camden—the Camden that I now know exists in every city in the entire world.

Lynne has begun to notice the invisible around her. Lynne has begun to see like Jesus.

It is cliché to say that the process of noticing the poor is not without difficulty and often pain. Many people—

especially those who are affluent—seldom make the effort to put themselves in situations where they will see beyond their own "gates." We tend to see only those who move within our own social circles. Richard Albert, a Franciscan priest who has worked in Kingston, Jamaica, for twenty-five years, expresses this difficulty. When he took a post at a middle-class parish, he vowed to break down the barriers that blinded some of the most comfortable. Albert writes, "The challenge for the modern Christian is not a matter of what profession you are in, but that you have to stand shoulder to shoulder with the poor. People in their Benzes and big cars pass through here (the slums) every day, but don't see behind the walls." Father Albert goes on to say, "You can't talk about meeting and talking with the Lord just in church. . . . You must bump into him, eat with him and cry with him in the poor."[3] Father Albert believes that if one encounters the poor, eats with them, and cries with them, then one might begin to respond in ways that help restore the poor to their full, God-intended humanity.

STORIES OF THE UNNOTICED NOTICED

Jesus was unique in that he noticed people whom most people walked past. Not only did Jesus notice people who had been excluded from his community, but he went out of his way to find them. He traveled in regions and areas where the unnoticed lived. One of the great challenges we face is becoming people who notice the forgotten and overlooked. It is very easy to live out our faith within the cloistered walls of our churches and gated communities. It takes an intentional commitment to move beyond our gates and see as Jesus saw. The following stories will, I hope, help you in the process of becoming a person whose eyes are opened to the broader realities of our world.

Crackers and Cranberries

We see from where we stand.

> Haitian proverb

"Why'd he keep asking me for crackers?" asked a puzzled Lynne.

It was warm that late September. Our principal was holding the weekly after-school teachers' meeting of our small, private high school. She had everyone's attention as she scrunched up her shoulders, tilted her head, and turned her palms outward in perplexity.

"Crackers?" she repeated, holding the pose for her captive audience. "Every morning around 8:50, just before first period," she continued, "Rudy would come to my office and politely ask me, 'Miss Lynne, do you have any of those crackers left?'

"The first couple of times I just thought he had brought some soup and wanted something to go with it. Then, just last week, I finally followed him down to his locker. No soup."

Great teachers are terrific detectives. The personal lives of their students are of genuine interest far beyond the walls of their classrooms. They intuitively pick up clues—any subtle shift in behavior. Driving to school, teacher-detectives think of their students; at the family dinner table, they talk about their students; as they lie in their beds, questions about their students rattle around in their minds. Was Tanya depressed today? Susan had a bruise over her left eye—what's happening at home? Terrance scored well below his average—why? These heroes of the classroom, teachers, carry the burden of their students' lives, trying to understand the negative forces that impact their classrooms.

"I casually started to ask Rudy some questions," continued our detective. "Turns out his mother leaves the house each morning at about six to pick cranberries in the bogs of

South Jersey. Therefore, it's Rudy's job to get his four younger brothers and sisters ready for school. Their electricity has been turned off for two weeks because of nonpayment, and one of the little brothers needs an electric respirator for his asthma."

We all sat stunned. Rudy? Not Rudy. He's the happy kid. Always smiling. Good grades. Courteous to a fault. How'd we miss this one?

"We knew things were difficult at Rudy's house, but *we just didn't know* the depth of the problem until the requests for crackers began to be repeated each morning," said Lynne with a tone of self-incrimination.

Why don't kids like Rudy just come out and say they're hungry or that their electricity has been off for a couple of weeks? They know our staff; we're like a family. They know that we never hesitate to help—but remember, it's awkward to be weak, to appear needy, to be dependent on other people, to be poor. Vulnerability is not the American way.

Our staff also knows that impoverished kids can be Academy Award winning actors. They appear at our programs dressed in ninety-five-dollar sneakers and designer jeans and look like they could fit into any upper-middle-class community in the country. Their outward appearance sends the message, "I'm cool. I'm not poor!" But the food cupboards are bare, the gas has been turned off, and the rent payments are two months in arrears.

Some critics respond to this "deception" by claiming that "those people" just need to get their priorities right. Those hundred-dollar sneakers could feed a family for a week, maybe two. The money used to purchase those designer jeans could have been used to buy pants for all the children. And the critics are right. Money could be used in more effective ways.

But what they fail to understand is the tremendous stigma attached to poverty—especially in America, where the very rich and the very poor share the universal space of television and shopping malls. The fact that images of affluence are beamed into the living rooms of the poor every night only heightens their pressure not to be seen as poor. Especially young people. They must confront the realities of peer pressure and peer cruelty; they are susceptible to the need to project a false front. It is humiliating to have anyone find out that you are poor.

I needed to hear Rudy's story for two reasons: I needed to be reminded that behind the facade of a handsome, vibrant, uniform-clad high school student was a young boy who came to school *hungry*! He probably had to share whatever food there was with his younger brothers and sisters so they could make it until their hot lunch program at school. And I needed to be reminded by the old saying that "all that glitters is not gold." I needed to intentionally look beyond the veneer of outward appearance and see some of the subtle changes in kids who walk through our school each day.

W. H. Auden wrote, "The first criterion of success in any human activity, the necessary preliminary, whether to scientific discovery or to artistic vision, is intensity of attention or, less pompously, love."[4] To understand what goes on in the lives of those with whom we work, minister, or live, we must *pay attention with intensity*. It is easy just to look but never really see.

The second reason I needed to hear Rudy's story was that raising money for the poor can actually desensitize us to the meaning of poverty. The *New York Times* has a section each Sunday detailing the glitter and beauty of the previous week's glamorous socialites, well coiffed and gowned, at charitable fund-raisers for the poor and needy.

And, alas, because I have the responsibility to raise funds for our programs, I too am frequently invited to dinners and golf outings and political receptions where I am served jumbo shrimp, flavored coffee, and an award-winning Cabernet Sauvignon to complement my rare filet mignon. I'm often taken to lunches and breakfasts by wealthy board members and contributors—good, sincere people who want to help the less fortunate. We talk, raise money, and advocate for the poor, but in the *doing* of those activities in posh clubs and eateries, it is easy to forget the *meaning* behind it all—what it feels like to be poor.

I have never had to beg for crackers. I do not have to spend emotional energy worrying about my next meal. Thus, I have difficulty imagining what it must be like to go through a day of school without food and know that it's likely I'll have no supper. The inability to feel what it is like to be poor worries me, for when we cannot feel something, we can blindly lose our way.

I wonder if the rich man in the biblical story failed to notice the poor man at his gate because he had never known what it was like to be hungry at the end of a day. The rich man was not bad—just a man desensitized to an experience outside his own. As Jesus told the story in Luke 16, the problem with the rich man was not that he was rich—for Lazarus was taken to the side of Abraham, one of the wealthier men in the Old Testament (see v. 22). The problem with the rich man was that *he did not notice.* He had a numbed awareness, a contentment that divorced him from the reality of people's poverty.

Yet Jesus calls us to *notice.* We are admonished to transcend our small worlds and take on the concerns of others. He stresses compassion—from the Latin words *com* ("with") and *passion* ("to feel"). To *feel with* others, in their difficult and debilitating circumstances, be they from Arizona or Zimbabwe, is the great biblical imperative. Only when we truly identify with another's suffering will we be compelled to act.

Many of us live in "gated communities." Our houses may not have real gates around them, but we have erected psychological gates between ourselves and those who are overlooked. I find I very easily drift into a kind of complacency where I fail to pick up on cues and notice those I need to notice. It takes a daily commitment and courage to move beyond our "gates"—whatever form those gates may take. We must be committed to looking to see what is out there. Reflect on your past week. Were there people you overlooked? Who do you need to notice?

Sacred Junk Mail

Lord, help me to do great things as though they were little, since I do them with your Power; and little things as though they were great, since I do them in your name.

Blaise Pascal

Jumping out of my Honda onto the asphalt parking lot, my eye was caught by something odd on the dashboard of the Ford Escort in the next space. I do not usually make a habit of peeping into the interiors of others' automobiles, but my peripheral vision caught something out of place. I pressed my face against the passenger window for closer examination.

I saw the aberration: taped to the dusty dashboard was a white three-by-five postcard—the kind of card hosting a small black-and-white photo of a child with the words "Have You Seen Me?" emblazoned across the bottom. At my house these little announcements are usually wedged between the shopper's guide and the Papa John's Pizza coupons. Frequently they are devoured by the clutches of the recycling bin after but a ceremonial glance to appease some subconscious trace of concern. Seldom do they find their way into the family reading pile. Never have they ended up on the dashboard of the family minivan.

Needless to say, I was surprised to see one of these little announcements swimming alone outside of the primordial sludge of Save-A-Lot flyers and back issues of the *New York Times*. It was strange. But right in front of me on the dashboard marquee was little seven-year-old Eddie Henderson's picture with "Call 1-800-THE-LOST" framing his smiling face. Eddie's picture had been saved from the recycle bin or the bottom of the kitty litter box to be mounted on the prime real estate of this family sedan—the dashboard.

I am a person who lives life at sixty-five miles per hour and rarely notices and contemplates the implications of what comes through my mailbox. Perhaps this is why the presence of this little card caught me so off guard. I had never really stopped to ponder what these little pictures, delivered to millions of mailboxes across the country, must mean to those who have lost a child. But to those who have had a child abducted, these pictures represent the last ray of hope that a stranger might spot their son or daughter—if people take the time to look. And the people who owned this little Ford Escort had taken the time.

I wondered briefly about the owners of this car. They may not have had an ostentatious Mercedes ornament mounted on their hood, but the display of junk mail on the dashboard spoke of their depth, their values, and their priorities.

How did the owners of this car become people who learned to care so deeply? Had they had a child who was abducted at some point? Had they known a friend or neighbor whose child went missing? Was little Eddie a friend of their child? Or were they people who refused to skim their way through life, people who instead engaged in the practice of notice and took time to care about little things—like intentionally taping up postcards of children whom they had never met and whom they would likely never find? Few people have the kind of faith to engage in this kind of intentional living.

I remember once hearing a radio interview with a Kenyan activist who had committed his life to fighting for freedom and challenging corrupt governments and corporations. He had been beaten, spent years in prison, and had family members killed because of his action. At one point in the discussion, the reporter conducting the interview said, "But you never stood a chance of changing things. The odds against you were so great. Why did you keep going?" His response was one I will never forgot. "Holy naïveté," laughed the man. "Like the prophets of old, you've got to be somewhat naive. It is the naïveté that allows you to move forward without being overwhelmed before you start."

The person who tapes postcards to the dashboard refuses to be defeated before the search begins. This person does not allow the exhausting and overwhelming junk mail barrage of airbrushed supermodels and two-for-one sales to drown out the face that truly needs to be noticed: the missing child.

Perhaps the postcard taping was naive. Perhaps this person had a "holy naïveté." But if it were *my* child on the postcard, I would hope for a whole world of people like the one in the parking space next to mine, all with dashboards reminding them to look for my son or daughter—to care. Wouldn't you?

This anonymous owner of the Ford Escort challenges me to feel with those parents who have lost their child. I know it is not really my responsibility to find the lost child of someone who lives in Arizona. And I know deep down that I will probably never find that child. Yet in the process of caring for someone I do not know, I somehow grow toward being the human God calls me to become. People are "invisible" to us because our hearts and eyes have not been transformed through repeated acts of noticing.

Whatever Happened to Ellie?

The biblical call to God's people is the same as it has always been: to choose life over death; to do justice, love mercy, and walk humbly with our God; to take our cross and follow Christ. Do we hear a new depth to that call in the rubble of destroyed skyscrapers, in the scorched earth of distant lands, in the cries of refugees? If we dare enter this most recent brutal crucifixion of the world, will we find our way to resurrection?

Will O'Brien

"One day I went in to work and Ellie wasn't there," my young friend Bob was telling me. Bob was a junior at a prestigious East Coast university. He was one of those ambitious young men who worked on the dish line just to make a few extra dollars to help with car payments. Ellie wasn't a student but had been in food services at the school for over twenty years. "So I asked around," he said, "and found out that Ellie'd had a heart attack and couldn't work anymore. What was worse, she didn't have health-care benefits or medical leave." Bob looked at me in total disbelief. "Can you believe that someone who works faithfully for twenty years gets sick and the university has no commitment to that person? That's wrong. *That's really wrong!*"

Raised in a middle-class home, Bob took things like health care for granted—when he got sick he went to the doctor, and when his parents got sick they took a few days off till they felt better. They *enjoyed* sick leave. Wasn't health care part of the American way of life? But sweating it out with Ellie in the dish line—he'd really come to like her—opened Bob's eyes to a whole new world.

"Well, I went to the administration," he said boastfully. "Can you believe it? They said they couldn't do anything for Miss Ellie Green. 'It's our policy,' was the answer they gave. *I was furious.* I went to visit Ellie. She had no income, and debts were piling up. She told me she couldn't afford to get the right medication. That was it! I decided to do something about it."

Bob described his crusade. "I wanted to do two things. One was to raise money to help Ellie cover her medical bills; the other was to put some heat on the administration. The first thing I did was to sponsor a dinner in Ellie's honor. I put flyers around the campus. I emailed friends. And guess what? The turnout was great! I was so pleased," he said with a wide smile, and he had good reason to be proud. "But then *I* had to speak." He paused for a moment and looked at me. "Do you ever get nervous speaking?" he asked as if he were looking for some reassurance.

"Sure, I get nervous," I said. "When I was your age I could hardly stand in front of people without losing my breath. I stumbled on half my words." Bob looked relieved to hear of my struggles.

"Well, I sure was nervous," he continued, now pacing the room. "I was shaking in my boots. But after I got going, I said some things that the students didn't want to hear, and I said some things that the administration didn't want to hear. I didn't want them just to put five dollars in the paper buckets that were passed around and feel that they had done their duty. I wanted people to understand that in our community of affluence, it was wrong for a person who had given her soul to the school to have to struggle because of her inability to work due to poor health.

"I think I made a few people angry. I was probably a bit over the top, but it was worth it, because everyone was exceptionally generous. They liked Ellie too. We took a collection at the dinner and raised over ten thousand dollars for her. Can you believe it? Ten thousand dollars!"

Bob went on to tell me that one of the highlights of his life was delivering the check to Ellie at her home. "She cried, and so did I," he admitted, "but you know what was really neat? A graduate student picked up on the issue of workmen's compensation and is working with the administration to revamp the benefits system for cafeteria workers. There's now some real hope for the future."

Bob is just one young student. He has no exceptional gifts. He certainly is not eloquent or charismatic as a leader. But something got under his skin. He sensed that an injustice had been committed, and he could not walk away; it would have violated his sense of what it meant to be a Christian.

We have all heard talk of a loving God, a powerful God, a sovereign God, a God of forgiveness and faithfulness. And, yes, these are central to God's character. But we must not overlook God's great attribute: justice.

I remember sitting on the dais at a conference with Jim Wallis, the founder of the Sojourners Community in Washington, DC. Speaker after speaker got up and talked about volunteering and helping people and doing all kinds of wonderful things in the name of God. Finally, Jim leaned over to me and whispered, "No one ever talks about justice. They just talk about charity."

As Christians we love to be involved in acts of charity, but how frequently do we engage ourselves in struggles for justice? There is a difference. Charity seldom changes a person's circumstances. It may put food in an empty stomach; it may provide a blanket for warmth. But charity does not attempt to *solve the problem* of hunger or homelessness.

Justice, on the other hand, attempts to change a person's circumstances. Justice asks the questions, Why is the person hungry? Why is the person cold? Justice seeks to change the systems that create the same oppressive situations day after day for people.

The prophet Micah cried out, "And what does the LORD require of you? To act justly and to love mercy and to walk humbly with your God" (Mic. 6:8 TNIV).

My friend Bob reminds me to go beyond charity. He challenges me to be a seeker of justice and see the issues that face those overlooked and invisible people who work hard but struggle for dignity.

Recently I read an interview with a Latino professor hired to work on faculty at a prominent American seminary. He was introduced by the president of the school as the first faculty member of Latin American ethnicity on staff. As soon as the professor took the podium, he corrected the president. "There are more than twenty people of Latin American descent on staff—they work as your gardeners, your janitors, and your cooks. But they are as much a part of this community as anybody else." His point was powerful. Many "invisible" people were working on campus. Do we notice those people around us who do not hold prominent titles and positions? Do we care about and speak up for the rights of people regardless of their place on the social ladder? This is justice. This is what it means to follow Jesus.

Tyrice: A Good Boy?

Once we take our eyes away from ourselves, from our interests, from our own rights, privileges, ambitions, then they will become clear to see Jesus around us.

Mother Teresa

What comes out of our mouths impacts the lives of others—and our own lives—in profound ways. Words sting and harm; words build up, restore, soothe, heal, and comfort. We've all heard—and used—words of love and words of hate. But do we sensitively and responsibly choose our words thoughtfully each time we open our mouths?

In the course of every day we are all choosing thousands of words as we constantly interact with people, saying things *to* them and *about* them. Seldom do we think about our words, but in spite of ourselves we are constantly making choices between bad words and good words: gossiping, cutting people down, demeaning others, spewing anger, cooing endearments, or lauding another with praise and adulation. Often we fail to really notice the situation and person, and we share an inappropriate word.

Take eight-year-old Tyrice Coleman, for instance. Tyrice was a young boy sitting three-quarters of the way up the aisle on the left side of our school bus. He was the last to get off on the route home and perched himself up on the back of the seat with his head out the open window. "You dumb geezers! You bunch of no-good old geezers," he yelled out the window at a group of older pedestrians sitting by the bus stop.

"You bums! You stupid drunks!" he screamed again with all the voice he could muster, this time flavoring his speech with a few unfortunate and inappropriate adjectives.

Had I been driving the bus, I would have slammed on the brakes, gotten in his face, and yelled at that little troublemaker in no uncertain terms to *sit down and shut your mouth*!

If that didn't get an instant response, I would have resorted to threats: "Do that again, buddy boy, and you won't come back to our program for a week!" Or the big one: "I'm going to talk to your mother!"

But our wiser, more thoughtful bus driver did none of the above. She had taken the time to understand what Tyrice really needed—she had truly noticed this little one.

In a display of holy wisdom, she simply cleared her throat, glanced in the overhead mirror, and said quietly, "Tyrice, good boys don't say unkind things. Good boys don't say unkind things."

For the next few moments there was only the deep hum of the bus rolling down a narrow street. Tyrice scrunched up his face, furrowed his eyebrows, crossed his arms, and contemplated the words of our driver.

At about 35th Street, Tyrice abruptly walked toward the front of the bus and took a seat just behind and across from the driver. "Ms. Gina, do you really think Tyrice is a good boy?"

"Of course he is," replied Gina without taking her eyes off the road. "Of course you're a good boy."

Tyrice got up from his seat, deliberately walked back down the aisle of the bus, and with the look of someone with a newfound revelation, mumbled, "Tyrice *is* a good boy. Tyrice is a *good* boy."

God's words, spoken through us, can transcend both our self-interests and our present emotional state. In difficult and tense situations, we *can* speak words that produce a sense of calmness and hope; when we are tired and frustrated, we *can* utter words that are not hurtful and damaging. In situations where truth needs to be spoken, we *can* utter necessary words without thinking of our self-interests.

You've probably heard the prayer often recited by pastors prior to a sermon: "May the words of my mouth and the meditation of my heart be pleasing in your sight, O LORD, my Rock and my Redeemer" (Ps. 19:14). It is a wonderful prayer and an important statement to make prior to sharing God's Word with a congregation. But what about our reciting that prayer prior to leaving our homes each morning?

Pastors pray the prayer before their sermons, elevating the importance of their words, but their words are no more important than the words we use, no more important than the words uttered by a bus driver to a child who had never been told that he was "a good boy."

A well-chosen word is like a "golden apple on a silver platter," says the author of Proverbs (25:11). How easy it would have been for Gina to miss the opportunity to share a redemptive word. How easy it would have been to overlook what this little boy really needed. How easy it would have been not to *notice* the deeper story of this little one. And yet a well-chosen word shared on a school bus, at home, at the office, or with our children can have a powerful, transforming, golden effect upon any life.

I often fail to see the "story behind the story." In the case of Tyrice, Gina was able to see a deeper issue and respond accordingly—a hurting boy needed attention. To view life and people as Gina viewed Tyrice takes a commitment to look at the world differently. When we begin to see people with sensitivity and understanding, we can respond in ways that are redemptive and ultimately healing.

Lord,
Teach us to notice those at our gates—those who
live outside the walls of our sometimes small vision.
May we hear the cries of those calling for mercy,
even when their cries are silent and our ears
    distracted.
And when we hear those cries,
fill our shoes with blocks of cement
so we will be inclined to stop.
Fill our hearts with the liquid of compassion
so we will be inclined to help.
Fill our hands with warmth and life
so we will pause to touch.
Amen.

12

CONCLUSION

Praying with Our Eyes Open

Go to chapel regularly; participate in the sacraments. In regular worship you can certainly expect to encounter God . . . but don't practice your prayer and worship as though they are somehow more sacred than or set apart from "ordinary life." God who is truth is the Creator who is truly present in all that is created, and in all people as their truest selves. Be quite certain, therefore, that when you truly encounter another human being and look with the eyes of wisdom and love you are not only seeing them in truth, you are truly seeing and meeting God in them. So pay attention, and never scorn or dismiss anybody as unimportant or unworthy of you.

Roberta Bondi[1]

A pastor friend tells a wonderful story of when, as a young man just out of seminary, he met the late Bryant Kirkland. Kirkland at that time was the highly regarded senior pastor at Fifth Avenue, and this up-and-coming pastor was to do an internship under his supervision. Their first meeting was lunch at the University Club in Manhattan—a rather auspicious start for the young seminarian.

When lunch arrived, Kirkland looked at the young seminarian and said, "Do you mind if we pray New York style?"

New York style? He had no idea what the older pastor was talking about, so he just nodded his head and smiled. At this Kirkland reached across the table, took his hand, and looked into his eyes. With his eyes wide open, he began to pray.

"Lord, thanks for my young friend. Thanks for the privilege of ministering with him. May our food today be as wonderful as our newfound friendship."

The prayer did not end. Kirkland began to look around the room. "And Lord, the waitress over there in the corner—she looks burdened. Please ease her burden. Give her something to smile about today." At this the young seminarian glanced over toward the corner. There was the waitress, looking somewhat burdened.

"And Lord, those businessmen and women at the table next to the window—as they make decisions over lunch that could potentially impact the lives of hundreds of people, help them make decisions with compassion and kindness."

For the next five minutes, Kirkland just looked around the University Club, making observations and praying for people *with his eyes wide open.*

Isn't this the way God wants us to live our lives—praying and living with our eyes wide open, noticing what God is doing through our neighbors, friends, co-workers, and life circumstances? Yet so many of us live our spiritual lives with our eyes closed, only opening them when we walk into church or some kind of "religious" event. I know it was true for me. For years I have prayed with my eyes closed, in darkness, separating my faith from the God activity that swirls around me every minute of the day. And yet I am discovering that this activity begs for my attention and my contemplation, because in this holy activity God wants to remind me how the heart of the gospel message can be lived faithfully in a complex and difficult world.

Please do not hear me wrong. I am not saying that we do not need times of isolation and solitude. In the Gospels we meet a Jesus who retreated to the mountains for prayer and solitude. But as Simon Carey Holt reminds us, "Jesus spends the largest part of his time in the most everyday settings,"[2] seemingly with his eyes wide open, noticing expressions of God's heart in the actions of others and identifying those sightings for his followers to embrace. And because of the way Jesus lived his life, we have vivid images of what it means to live with compassion, love, sacrifice, contrition, faith, courage, gratitude, and humility. Because of Jesus, we can look for these same vivid images of faithfulness in our lives today, drawing inspiration and courage to exercise similar behaviors in our own lives.

But this is a difficult step. It takes a new way of looking at life

CHOOSING WHAT WE HEAR

Some of you may still be saying, "That's impossible. I am surrounded by bad news constantly. There is no good news to see, let alone emulate!" Perhaps this is true. But I wonder if you have tried to practice the discipline of noticing.

I remember a story I heard as a teenager. It was used as an illustration in one of those sermons I had forgotten before I sang the last hymn. The sermon was lost, but the story stuck.

The United Nations held a conference in New York City. People from all over the world had gathered to discuss issues pertinent to globalization. During a lunch break, two participants decided to walk around the busy streets of New York and grab a deli sandwich. One of the men was a Native

American and had spent his early years learning the ways of the wilderness. He had tracked animals, scaled mountains, and canoed beautiful lakes.

New York City was its usual hectic potpourri of sirens, ringing cell phones, honking cars, and blaring radios. People were yelling for cabs. Music was drifting out of windows. New York was alive in all its glory, chaos, and splendor. As the two walked down Fifth Avenue, the Native American turned abruptly to the other man and said, "Did you hear that?"

"Hear what?" laughed the other.

"That cricket. Did you hear that cricket?"

"You can't hear a cricket in this noise," said the other delegate impatiently.

The Native American slowly walked over to a discarded paper cup lying on the sidewalk. He bent down and picked up a little brown cricket from inside.

"That's amazing," said the first man in total disbelief. "How did you do that?"

"It's really not that difficult. One hears what one wants to hear."

"Oh, come on," began the other. "All this deafening noise. All this chaos. No, no. You've got a gift."

The Native American was not about to gloat about his accomplishment. "Watch this," he continued, trying to make his point. He took a handful of coins out of his pocket, raised his hand, and dropped the coins on the sidewalk. When the change hit the pavement, the coins made tinny chinking sounds as they hit the sidewalk in front of Saks Fifth Avenue.

Every pedestrian within thirty-five feet of them stopped dead in their tracks for a moment and turned toward the two men.

"You see what I mean," smiled the Native American. "We notice what we are attuned to notice."

A NEW WAY TO NOTICE

Every time I reflect on that story, I smile because I know it to be true. As people of the twenty-first century, we are attuned to certain things. The attuning becomes instinctual. An automatic reaction. In the deep recesses of our minds we are attuned to certain sounds and certain sights. We see and hear what we have been trained to see and hear. And the media are massively influential in shaping the diet that nurtures our souls. As God's people, however, the challenge for us is to retrain our eyes, our hearts, and our ears to intuitively see and hear behaviors that reflect the heart and nature of God in our world. For in our ability to nurture these images we will find our ability to live more faithfully and passionately in our world.

Perhaps this is why it is helpful to go back a few centuries and glean insight from two writers who challenged their contemporaries to live their spiritual lives differently. Saint Ignatius of Loyola and Saint Benedict can help us as we try to live a noticed life in the twenty-first century. Saint Ignatius lived back in the 1400s and initiated the Jesuit movement. He instructed his followers to develop a discipline called the *examane of conscience*, an exercise that challenged people to reflect on life as they were living it, looking for God's movement and involvement in the rough-and-tumble of everyday life. Spirituality, for Ignatius, was not simply a twenty-minute devotional at the beginning of the day. Rather, it was a reflective process attempting to find God in the mix of all of life. Ignatius believed that God was always breaking through into ordinary reality—we simply miss this God-involvement because we have not trained our eyes to see and ears to hear. Simply put, Ignatius tried to get his followers to open their eyes, ears, and hearts and notice the presence of God in all aspects of their daily lives. At the end of each day, Ignatius would reflect upon *every* moment of his day—like examining the individual frames of a motion picture—looking for God's Spirit and trying to discern what God was teaching him in each encounter and episode. By finding God's relentless presence in the ordinary places of his life, Ignatius found nourishment in the evidences of God's love and grace in the minute details of his day.

Saint Benedict, on the other hand, emphasized that there should be no separation between work and our spiritual lives. The spirituality that emerges from *The Rule of Saint Benedict* is charged with living the ordinary life extraordinarily well. Transforming daily life, rather than transcending it, is what really mattered to Saint Benedict. *The Rule of Saint Benedict* is meant for hardworking, busy people who have families, pay bills, and participate in civic duties. It is a working person's spirituality.

Joan Chittister, whom I mentioned earlier in this book and who writes wonderful material on the Benedictine life, adds, "Most of us must simply live where we are, in the midst of the crowds and the complex questions. Most of us have no other access to God and the good life except now, except here. The problem becomes discovering how to make here and now, right and holy for us. The here and now is all we have, any of us, out of which to make life worthwhile and God present and holiness a normal, rather than an unnatural, way of life."[3] This was Benedict's quest—helping people like you and me to make the here and now holy! One practice of the Benedictines that was especially meaningful in helping the monks develop this discipline was for the abbey bells to ring each hour. It reminded the monks to say a little prayer and begin the search to find the presence of God in their labor and interactions with the other brothers. Whether they were pulling weeds, washing dishes, baking bread, or eating a communal meal, all was considered sacred because it was done in the presence of God.

What both these saints affirm is that we need not separate the normal aspects of daily life and our ability to enrich our lives spiritually. For God is not just someone to relate to when we have a few free moments of undistracted time in a chapel or prayer closet. Rather, God is ever-present and moving in the midst of all daily life. We just need to learn the discipline of *noticing* these little eruptions of God's activity in the routines, the pain, and the chaos of our day. And those bursts of divine grace, love, and creativity come in many forms. They may find expression in the comments of a friend or a stranger. They may find expression in the compassionate acts of an employee in the workplace. They may find expression in a miraculous act of gracious provision: a smiling child or a prophetic word. These bursts of *God-activity* may even be found in the presence of a dying friend.

When I began to believe I could potentially find the presence of God in different ways and in different places, my life changed. Rather than trying to access a God who was *outside* of life, I began to see that God does not need to be accessed—God is already present, trying to access me. When I made this shift, suddenly traces of God began to appear in places and situations I never could have imagined them. I began to see that God's revelation is not simply limited to the pages of Scripture. Rather, God wants to teach me daily with fresh revelations in unlikely places and through unlikely people. I have begun to realize that God wants to teach me new things—right here, right now.

For many people this kind of spiritual feeding may seem like a stretch—subjective, postmodern, and potentially self-serving. I can hear the skeptics saying, "I need objective truth grounded in God's Word!" I do not refute the importance of good biblical study, as Scripture often becomes the lens through which our experiences of God are validated. But to limit our spiritual diet to daily devotions and a weekly sermon is to assert that God is no longer at work in the world and that God speaks only in certain places and at certain times.

This was illustrated by a man who approached me one day after church. I had been the guest preacher that morning, so he met me in the receiving line during coffee hour. After shaking my hand he looked into my eyes and said, "You know, I just love Sunday." He paused for a moment and then continued, "I just love coming to church. I get so spiritually charged that it helps me endure the monotony of my week. I wish we had church every day!" I am glad he enjoyed church so much, but I found his comments somewhat tragic. This man had his spiritual life on Sunday—a life full of the things of God. And then he had his daily life—a life devoid of meaning and barren of God's presence. I was sad that his Monday-to-Saturday life could not have been as spiritually "charged" as Sunday. I was sad he could not begin to practice a life noticed.

This is our challenge as people who spend most of our lives in "the world." We need to cultivate the practice of noticing so that Monday through Saturday will not be viewed as a wasteland, devoid of spiritual meaning and significance.

Let us begin today to learn to *live with our eyes open*.

Try to listen more intently.

Try to discern what God is doing around you.

Make every moment of your life a prayer.

NOTES

Introduction

1. Jeffery Gettleman, "Camden's Streets Go from Mean to Meanest," *New York Times*, December 29, 2004.

Chapter 1: Beginning the Practice of Notice

1. Dolores Leckey, *Seven Essentials of the Spiritual Journey* (New York: Crossroad, 1999).

2. Ray Bradbury, *Fahrenheit 451* (New York: Ballantine Books, 1991), 9.

3. I direct an inner-city ministry called UrbanPromise that seeks to equip children and teens in underresourced communities with the skills necessary for academic achievement, life management, spiritual growth, and Christian leadership. Urban-Promise works in Camden, NJ; Wilmington, DE; Toronto, ON; and Vancouver, BC. Please visit www.urbanpromiseusa.org.

4. Frederick Buechner, *The Longing for Home: Recollections and Reflections* (San Francisco: HarperSanFrancisco, 1996), 111.

Chapter 2: Jesus and the Practice of Notice

1. Simon Carey Holt, "Finding God in the Ordinary, the Mundane, and the Immediate," *Theology, News and Notes*, March 1999, 13.

2. Don Postma, *Space for God: The Study and Practice of Prayer and Spirituality* (Grand Rapids: Bible Way, 1985), 102.

Chapter 4: Gratitude Noticed

1. Dennis Hamm, SJ, "What the Samaritan Leper Sees: The Narrative Christology of Luke 17:11–19," *Catholic Biblical Quarterly* 56, no. 1 (1994): 278.

2. Duncan M. Derret, "Gratitude and the Ten Lepers," *The Downside Review* 113, no. 390 (1995): 84.

3. Frederick J. Gaiser, "'Your Faith Has Made You Well': Healing and Salvation in Luke 17:12–19," *Word and World* 16, no. 3 (1996): 295.

4. Henri Nouwen, *The Return of the Prodigal Son* (New York: Doubleday, 1992), 85.

5. Stephen L. Carter, "A Politics of Gratitude," *Christianity Today*, March 2004, 74.

6. Ibid.

7. Ibid.

Chapter 5: Children Noticed

1. Judith Gundry-Volf, "To Such as These Belongs the Reign of God," *Theology Today* 56, no. 4 (January 2000): 472.

2. Ibid., 473.

3. Ibid., 475.

4. Joan Chittister, *Wisdom Distilled from the Daily: Living the Rule of St. Benedict Today* (San Francisco: HarperSanFrancisco, 1991), 54.

5. Gundry-Volf, "To Such as These," 479.

6. Jürgen Moltmann, "Child and Childhood as Metaphors of Hope," *Theology Today* 56, no. 4 (January 2000): 601.

7. Eugene Peterson, "Transparent Lives," *The Christian Century*, November 29, 2003, 22.

Chapter 6: Compassion Noticed

1. Henri J. M. Nouwen, Donald P. McNeill, Douglas A. Morrison, *Compassion: A Reflection on the Christian Life* (New York: Image Books, 1983), 4.

2. Ibid.

3. Thomas Merton, "Marxism and Monastic Perspectives," in *A New Charter of Monasticism*, ed. John Moffitt (Notre Dame, IN: University of Notre Dame Press, 1970), 80.

4. Samuel P. Oliner and Pearl M. Oliner, *The Altruistic Personality: Rescuers of Jews in Nazi Europe* (New York: Free Press, 1988), 174–75.

5. Meister Eckhart, quoted in Matthew Fox, *Original Blessing* (New York: Jeremy P. Tarcher/Putnam, 1983), 277.

Chapter 7: Courage Noticed

1. Ruby Sales, "Somebody Touched Me," *The Other Side*, November/December 2003, 10.

2. Ibid., 12.

3. Maya Angelou, "An Interview," *Third Way*, December 2002, 18.

Chapter 8: Contrition Noticed

1. Mikeal C. Parsons, "'Short in Stature': Luke's Physical Description of Zacchaeus," *New Testament Studies* 47 (January 2001) (New York: Cambridge University Press): 57.

2. Walter Brueggemann, *Reverberations of Faith: A Theological Handbook of Old Testament Themes* (Louisville: Westminster John Knox, 2002), 185.

3. Diogenes Allen, *Spiritual Theology: The Theology of Yesterday for Spiritual Help Today* (Cambridge, MA: Cowley, 1997), 9.

4. Ibid.

5. Ibid., 8.

6. Miroslav Volf, "The Social Meaning of Reconciliation," *Interpretation* 54, no. 2 (April 2000): 171.

7. J. Heinrich Arnold, *Discipleship: Living for Christ in the Daily Grind* (Farmington, PA: Plough, 1994), xix.

8. C. S. Lewis, *Mere Christianity* (San Francisco: HarperSanFrancisco, 2001), 121–22.

9. Chittister, *Wisdom Distilled from the Daily*, 64.

Chapter 9: Faith Noticed

1. Peter J. Gomes, *The Good Life: Truths That Last in Times of Need* (San Francisco: HarperSanFrancisco, 2002), 267.

Chapter 10: Sacrifice Noticed

1. Mary Anderson, "The Widow's Walk," *Christian Century*, November 1, 2003, 18.

2. Ibid.

Chapter 11: The Unnoticed Noticed

1. Charles H. Talbert, *Reading Luke: A Literary and Theological Commentary on the Third Gospel* (New York: Crossroad, 1982), 157.

2. Shane Claiborne, "Downward Mobility in an Upscale World," *The Other Side*, November–December 2000, 11.

3. David Gonzales, "Bronx Priest Fights for Jamaica's Poor," *New York Times*, November 22, 2001.

4. W. H. Auden, *The English Auden: Poems, Essays, and Dramatic Writings, 1927–1939*, ed. Edward Mendelssohn (New York: Random House, 1977), 319.

Chapter 12: Conclusion: Praying with Our Eyes Open

1. Roberta Bondi, "Back to School with Julian of Norwich: God 101," *Christian Century*, August 28, 2002, 20–21.

2. Holt, "Finding God in the Ordinary," 13.

3. Chittister, *Wisdom Distilled from the Daily*, 7.

Bruce Main is a graduate of Azusa Pacific University and Fuller Theological Seminary and holds a Doctor of Ministry degree from Princeton Theological Seminary. He speaks both nationally and internationally at colleges, conferences, and churches and has written several books, including *If Jesus Were a Sophomore* and *Revolution and Renewal* (with Tony Campolo). He is also the founding executive director of UrbanPromise Ministries, which seeks to equip inner-city children and teens with the skills necessary for academic achievement, life management, spiritual growth, and Christian leadership in Camden, New Jersey; Wilmington, Delaware; Toronto, Ontario; and Vancouver, British Columbia. This mission is fulfilled through after-school programs, summer camps, job training initiatives, alternative schools, small business development, college internships, teen parent programs, and a host of additional initiatives. Bruce is married with three children and lives in New Jersey. Additional information can be found at www.urbanpromiseusa.org.

Interested in sharing your own
"*spotting the sacred*" moments
and learning where others
spot the sacred in their lives?.

www.spottingthesacred.com

is the place to share your stories and pictures.
Author Bruce Main will also provide tips on how
to better see God in the world around you.

Join the community that looks for God in the
big and small moments of life, and be transformed!

"Without a doubt, UrbanPromise is one of the best urban ministries in the United States."

—**Tony Campolo**

"UrbanPromise is one of the best faith-based grassroots organizations I have ever seen and an inspiring example of how the love of Christ can hit the streets."

—**Jim Wallis**, author, *God's Politics*; founder, *Sojourners* magazine

In 1988 Bruce Main opened the doors of UrbanPromise in Camden, New Jersey, and began an after-school program with forty eager children. That summer UrbanPromise also hosted two summer camps in the city with over one hundred children attending. Main believed that the youth of Camden deserved a safe place to go after school and in the summer, quality education, job training, and mentoring.

Today UrbanPromise is directly involved in the lives of over seven hundred children and teens across the city. UrbanPromise is comprised of the following components:

- **The Camden Forward School**, a Christian-based elementary and middle school where over 120 of Camden's children receive an education in a safe and loving environment.

- **The UrbanPromise Academy**, a private high school focusing on the needs of teens who are not realizing their academic potential in public education.

- **After-School Programs and Summer Camps**, creative, structured programs committed to providing a safe and loving place for over five hundred children to come after school and during the summer to realize their God-given abilities.

- **The StreetLeader Program**, a program training and employing over one hundred local teens to work as mentors, teachers, and counselors to the children in the after-school programs and summer camps.

If you would like more information, please contact:

UrbanPromise Ministries
P.O. Box 1479, Camden, NJ 08105
T: (856) 661-1700 • F: (856) 661-1954
www.urbanpromiseusa.org